ANDALUC
TRAVEL GUIDE

2024 Edition

Wanderlust in Andalucia: Uncover Hidden Gems and Local Secrets

Jim Baxter

All rights reserved. No part of this book may be reproduced, stored in a retrieval system, or transmitted in any form or by any means, electronic, mechanical, photocopying, recording, or otherwise, without the prior written permission of the copyright owner. The information contained in this book is for general information purposes only. The author and publisher make no representations or warranties of any kind, express or implied, about the completeness, accuracy, reliability, suitability or availability with respect to the book or the information, products, services, or related graphics contained in the book for any purpose. Any reliance you place on such information is therefore strictly at your own risk.

Copyright © 2023 by Jim Baxter.

TABLE OF CONTENT

Introduction _____ 7
Unveiling the Riches of Southern Spain _____ 9
   The History and Heritage of Andalucia _____ 9
   Exploring Andalucia's Cultural Diversity _____ 11
   Iconic Landmarks and Must-Visit Cities _____ 14
   Practical Tips for Traveling in Andalucia _____ 22
      Best Time to Visit: _____ 22
      Transportation: _____ 24
      Accommodation _____ 28
      Local Customs and Etiquette: _____ 36
      Safety Considerations: _____ 38
   Language _____ 41
      Local Events and Festivals: _____ 43
      Exploring Off the Beaten Path: _____ 46
      Local Recommendations: _____ 50

Discovering the Soul of Andalucia: A Journey through Time and Culture _____ 55
   Delving into Andalucia's Moorish Legacy _____ 55
   Tracing the Footsteps of Flamenco _____ 58
   Embracing Andalucia's Gastronomic Traditions _____ 60
   Immersing in Local Festivals and Traditions _____ 63

Immerse Yourself in Andalucia: A Comprehensive Travel Companion _____ 67
   Planning Your Itinerary: From Coastal Charms to Inland Treasures _____ 67
   Navigating Andalucia's Transportation System _____ 69
   Accommodation Options and Recommendations _____ 72

Essential Travel Tips for Safety and Comfort _____ 75

From Flamenco to Tapas: Embrace the Essence of Andalucia _____ 85

Exploring Andalucia's Vibrant Culinary Scene _____ 85

Sampling Traditional Tapas and Local Delicacies __ 88

Sipping Andalucian Wines and Spirits _____ 91

Experiencing Flamenco: Music, Dance, and Passion 94

Unforgettable Adventures Await: Exploring Andalucia's Natural Wonders _____ 99

The Sierra Nevada: Hiking and Skiing in the South _ 99

Coastal Charms: Beaches and Water Activities _____ 101

Discovering Andalucia's National Parks and Biosphere Reserves _____ 104

Outdoor Excursions: Cycling, Horseback Riding, and More _____ 106

Beyond the Alhambra: Unlocking Andalucia's Architectural Gems _____ 111

The Alcazar of Seville: A Royal Retreat _____ 111

The Great Mosque of Cordoba: A Testament to Islamic Architecture _____ 113

The Cathedral of Malaga: Gothic Grandeur _____ 116

Ronda's Puente Nuevo: The Bridge to Andalucia's Past _____ 118

Tantalizing Tastes and Vibrant Festivals: A Taste of Andalucia's Culinary Delights _____ 123

Andalucian Gastronomy: A Fusion of Flavors _____ 123

The Feria de Abril: Seville's Flamboyant Spring Fair 125

Semana Santa: Andalucia's Holy Week Celebrations 128

The Cordoba Patio Festival: Floral Beauty and
Tradition_____131

*Wanderlust in Andalucia: Uncover Hidden Gems and
Local Secrets* _____*135*

Off the Beaten Path: Andalucia's Hidden Villages ___135

Insider Tips for Authentic Experiences _____138

Unique Souvenirs to Bring Home _____141

Andalucia's Best-Kept Secrets: Unraveling Local
Legends and Mysteries_____144

*Conclusion*_____*147*

Appendix: Useful Resources and Further Reading: _149

Important Note Before You Continue Reading

Unlock a World of Wonder: Embrace the Uncharted Beauty of Andalucía

Step into a realm where extraordinary experiences lie within the pages of this exceptional travel guide. Our mission is simple: to ignite your imagination, fuel your creativity, and awaken the daring adventurer within you. Unlike conventional guides, we choose to forgo images, as we firmly believe in the power of firsthand discovery—unfiltered and uninfluenced by preconceptions. Prepare yourself for an enchanting voyage, where each monument, every corner, and every hidden gem eagerly await your personal encounter. Why spoil the exhilaration of that first glimpse, that overwhelming sense of awe? Get ready to embark on an unparalleled journey, where the vessel propelling you forward is none other than your boundless imagination, and you will be the architect of your own destiny. Abandon any preconceived notions and find yourself transported to an authentic Andalucía, a realm teeming with extraordinary revelations. Brace yourself, for the magic of this expedition begins now, and remember, the most breathtaking images will be the ones painted by your own eyes.

In stark contrast to traditional guides, this book rejects the need for detailed maps. Why, you ask? Because we fervently believe that the greatest discoveries occur when you lose yourself, when you surrender to the ebb and flow of your surroundings, and embrace the thrill of the unknown path. No predetermined itineraries, no precise directions—our intention is to liberate you, allowing you to explore Andalucía on your terms, without boundaries or limitations. Surrender to the currents and unveil hidden treasures that no map could ever reveal. Embrace audacity, follow your instincts, and prepare to be astounded. The magic of this expedition commences in your world without maps, where roads materialize with each step, and the most extraordinary adventures await within the unexplored folds of the unknown.

Introduction

Welcome to the enchanting region of Andalucia, where history, culture, and natural beauty blend seamlessly to create a truly captivating travel destination. Nestled in the southern part of Spain, Andalucia is a land of contrasts, where ancient Moorish architecture meets vibrant flamenco rhythms, and where sun-soaked beaches coexist with rugged mountain ranges. This Andalucia Travel Guide is your passport to unraveling the riches of this remarkable region, providing you with the knowledge and inspiration to embark on an unforgettable journey.

Andalucia is steeped in a rich tapestry of history and heritage. From its Moorish past to its Roman and Phoenician influences, the region boasts a fascinating mix of cultures and civilizations that have left an indelible mark. Explore the magnificent Alhambra in Granada, an architectural masterpiece adorned with intricate tilework and serene courtyards. Walk through the ancient streets of Seville, where Gothic cathedrals stand in grandeur next to medieval palaces. And witness the grandeur of the Great Mosque of Cordoba, a symbol of Andalucia's Islamic legacy.

But Andalucia is not just about its historical treasures. It is a region that pulsates with life, where the rhythm of flamenco fills the air and the aromas of tantalizing tapas waft through bustling streets. Immerse yourself in the passion and soul of flamenco, the traditional music and dance that originated in Andalucia. Indulge in the region's gastronomic delights, savoring the rich flavors of traditional dishes like gazpacho, paella, and the famous jamón ibérico. And be sure to join in the festivities during Semana Santa or the Feria de Abril, where the streets come alive with color, music, and vibrant celebrations.

As you navigate your way through Andalucia, this travel guide will serve as your faithful companion, providing you with comprehensive information on planning your itinerary, getting around, and choosing the best accommodations. Discover the hidden gems and local secrets that lie off the beaten path, where you can immerse yourself in the authentic charm of Andalucian villages and connect with the warm and welcoming locals.

Whether you're a history enthusiast, a food lover, a nature explorer, or simply a wanderer in search of new experiences, Andalucia has something to offer every traveler. From the snow-capped peaks of the Sierra Nevada to the sun-kissed beaches of the Costa del Sol, from the vibrant cities to the tranquil countryside, this region will captivate your senses and leave an indelible mark on your soul.

So, embark on this journey with us as we unveil the wonders of Andalucia. Let this guide be your key to unlocking the treasures of this extraordinary region, where centuries-old traditions meet modern-day marvels, and where the spirit of Andalucia will embrace you with its warmth and beauty. Get ready to create memories that will last a lifetime as you explore Andalucia's history, indulge in its flavors, and immerse yourself in its vibrant culture. Your adventure awaits!

Unveiling the Riches of Southern Spain

The History and Heritage of Andalucia

Andalucia, the southernmost region of Spain, is a captivating destination that showcases a remarkable history and rich cultural heritage. This region has been shaped by the influence of numerous civilizations that have left an indelible mark on its landscapes and traditions. By delving into Andalucia's past, we can unravel the fascinating layers of history that have molded the region into what it is today.

One of the earliest civilizations to leave their imprint on Andalucia were the Phoenicians. These seafaring traders from the eastern Mediterranean established colonies along the coast, bringing with them their unique cultural practices and trade networks. The city of Cadiz, founded by the Phoenicians around 1100 BC, stands as a testament to their presence in the region. Explore the ancient ruins and discover the remnants of their commercial and cultural influence.

Following the Phoenicians, the Carthaginians arrived in Andalucia, establishing their dominance in the 6th century BC. They too contributed to the region's cultural tapestry, leaving traces of their influence in cities like Cartagena and Malaga. As you wander through the historical sites and museums, you can uncover the stories of ancient battles and the interplay between civilizations.

However, it was the Romans who truly left an enduring mark on Andalucia. With their conquest of the Iberian Peninsula in the 3rd century BC, they brought their advanced infrastructure, governance systems, and architectural prowess to the region. Explore the well-preserved Roman ruins of Italica near Seville, where you can walk amidst the remnants of a grand amphitheater, public baths, and the birthplace of two Roman emperors.

The fall of the Roman Empire saw the emergence of the Visigoths, who established their kingdom in Andalucia. Although their rule was relatively short-lived, lasting from the 6th to the 8th century AD, they played a significant role in shaping the region's medieval history. Explore the remnants of Visigothic architecture in the city of Toledo, where you can witness the fusion of Visigothic and Moorish influences.

The most transformative period in Andalucia's history was undoubtedly the arrival of the Moors from North Africa. Beginning in the 8th century AD, the Moors, led by the Umayyad caliphate, embarked on the conquest of the Iberian Peninsula. Their rule lasted for over seven centuries and brought about a golden age of art, architecture, and intellectual pursuit. The city of Cordoba became a center of learning and cultural exchange, boasting the magnificent Great Mosque, now known as the Mezquita, which showcases the intricate beauty of Moorish architecture.

The jewel of Andalucia during the Moorish period was undoubtedly the city of Granada. It was here that the Nasrid dynasty established the last Muslim stronghold on the peninsula. The Alhambra, a UNESCO World Heritage site, stands as a testament to the opulence and architectural brilliance of the Nasrid rulers. Its intricate courtyards, lush gardens, and intricate stonework transport visitors to a bygone era of Moorish grandeur.

Throughout Andalucia, you can witness the interplay of various cultures and architectural styles. From the Roman columns and aqueducts that have stood the test of time to the mesmerizing Alcazar of Seville, which showcases a fusion of Moorish and Christian influences, the region is a living museum of historical and architectural treasures.

As you explore the historic cities of Andalucia, such as Seville, Granada, Cordoba, Malaga, and Ronda, you'll find yourself immersed in a vibrant tapestry of cultural exchange. The winding streets, lively plazas, and enchanting neighborhoods bear witness to centuries of conquest, trade, and coexistence.

Beyond the cities, the rural landscapes of Andalucia also hold hidden gems. White-washed villages, perched on hilltops, offer a glimpse into the region's rural traditions and a slower pace of life. These picturesque towns, like Arcos de la Frontera, Vejer de la Frontera, and Frigiliana, provide a window into the authentic Andalusian way of life.

Andalucia's captivating history and cultural heritage have made it a truly unique destination. By venturing through its ancient ruins, wandering its streets, and embracing its traditions, you can unravel the layers of civilizations that have shaped this enchanting region. And as you do, you'll come to appreciate the diverse tapestry of influences that make Andalucia a must-visit destination for history buffs and culture enthusiasts alike.

Exploring Andalucia's Cultural Diversity

Andalucia, known as a melting pot of cultures, is a region in southern Spain that exudes a vibrant and unique cultural tapestry. Throughout history, diverse influences from different civilizations have fused together, resulting in a rich and captivating cultural diversity that defines Andalucia today. In this section, we invite you to immerse yourself in the traditions, art forms, and celebrations that make Andalucia an extraordinary destination.

One of the most iconic and renowned aspects of Andalusian culture is flamenco. Flamenco is a passionate and expressive art form that combines music, dance, and singing. It originated from the fusion of various cultural influences, including Romani, Moorish, and Spanish Gypsy traditions. Experience the mesmerizing rhythms of flamenco, as the soulful guitar strums, the haunting melodies of the singer, and the intricate footwork of the dancers create an enchanting and emotional atmosphere. Witnessing a live flamenco performance is an absolute must during your visit to Andalucia, as it allows you to immerse yourself in the intensity and authenticity of this unique art form.

In addition to flamenco, Andalucia is known for its traditional Andalusian music, which carries a distinct flavor and charm. The melodies and rhythms of traditional music in Andalucia reflect the region's diverse cultural influences, blending Moorish, Sephardic Jewish, and Christian elements. From the soul-stirring sounds of the flamenco guitar to the vibrant beats of the castanets and tambourines, Andalusian music captivates the heart and transports you to a different time and place. Take the opportunity to attend a live music performance, where talented musicians showcase the rich musical heritage of Andalucia, and let the melodies resonate within you.

Another cultural aspect that holds a significant place in Andalusian tradition is the art of bullfighting. While it may be a controversial topic, bullfighting has deep historical and cultural roots in Andalucia. It is a spectacle that has been practiced for centuries, serving as a symbol of bravery, tradition, and artistic expression. To fully understand the cultural significance of bullfighting, consider attending a bullfight at one of Andalucia's renowned bullrings. Experience the thrill and tension as the matador and the bull engage in a dramatic dance of courage and skill. The elaborate costumes, the pageantry, and the music add to the theatrical ambiance, offering a glimpse into the passion and complexity of this traditional Andalusian art form.

In addition to flamenco, traditional music, and bullfighting, Andalucia is home to a plethora of other cultural celebrations and festivities. The region hosts numerous festivals throughout the year, each offering a unique and immersive experience. One of the most famous festivals in Andalucia is the Feria de Abril in Seville. This week-long celebration showcases the region's vibrant spirit, with locals donning traditional attire, dancing Sevillanas (a traditional dance), and enjoying music, food, and drink in the decorated casetas (marquees). The Semana Santa (Holy Week) processions in cities like Seville, Malaga, and Granada are another significant cultural event. During Semana Santa, religious brotherhoods carry intricate floats depicting scenes from the Passion of Christ through the streets, accompanied by haunting music and solemn processions. These festivals provide a glimpse into the deeply rooted traditions and customs that have been passed down through generations in Andalucia.

Andalucia's cultural diversity extends beyond music and celebrations. The region's architecture, arts, and crafts also reflect the fusion of different influences. Marvel at the intricate details and exquisite beauty of Moorish architecture in landmarks such as the Alhambra in Granada and the Mezquita in Cordoba. The grandeur of these architectural wonders serves as a testament to the region's rich cultural heritage. Andalucia is also known for its vibrant and colorful ceramics, handmade pottery, and intricate tilework, which can be found in the local markets and artisan workshops. Exploring these art forms allows you to appreciate the craftsmanship and artistic traditions that have been cherished in Andalucia for centuries.

As you delve into the cultural diversity of Andalucia, you will witness the dynamic interplay of different influences that have shaped the region's identity. The traditions, art forms, and celebrations in Andalucia offer a window into the vibrant soul of the region. Embrace the passionate rhythms of flamenco, be moved by the melodies of traditional music, witness the spectacle of a bullfight, and immerse yourself in the festivities that bring communities together. Allow Andalucia to captivate your senses, leaving you with a deep appreciation for the cultural richness that thrives in this extraordinary part of southern Spain.

Iconic Landmarks and Must-Visit Cities

Andalucia, with its wealth of historical and architectural treasures, beckons travelers to immerse themselves in its vibrant tapestry of landmarks and cities. Each destination showcases a unique aspect of the region's rich heritage, inviting visitors to delve deeper into the wonders of Andalucia. In this section, we will explore three iconic landmarks and must-visit cities that epitomize the historical and architectural splendors of Andalucia: the Alhambra in Granada, the Mezquita in Cordoba, and the city of Seville.

The Majestic Alhambra in Granada:

Nestled against the backdrop of the Sierra Nevada Mountains, the Alhambra stands as a testament to the beauty and grandeur of Moorish architecture. This awe-inspiring palace complex is a UNESCO World Heritage site and one of the most visited attractions in Spain.

As you wander through the Alhambra, you will be captivated by its intricate carvings, ornate tilework, and serene courtyards. Explore the Nasrid Palaces, where you can marvel at the delicate plasterwork of the Mexuar, the stunning Court of the Lions with its iconic fountain, and the mesmerizing beauty of the Palace of the Lions. The Generalife Gardens, with their lush greenery, fragrant flowers, and stunning views, provide a tranquil oasis within the palace complex.

The Awe-Inspiring Mezquita in Cordoba:

In the heart of Cordoba lies the Mezquita, a masterpiece that combines both Islamic and Christian architectural styles. Originally built as a mosque during the Moorish rule, it was later converted into a cathedral after the Reconquista. This remarkable blend of cultures and religions makes the Mezquita a symbol of Cordoba's historical significance and cultural diversity.

Step inside the Mezquita and be greeted by the breathtaking forest of columns and arches that stretch as far as the eye can see. Wander through the prayer hall, adorned with red-and-white double arches, and discover the remarkable Mihrab, a masterpiece of Islamic craftsmanship. The Christian additions, including the Renaissance-style cathedral within the mosque, add yet another layer of intrigue and beauty to this architectural marvel.

The Enchanting Streets of Seville:

Seville, the capital of Andalucia, is a city that brims with charm and history. Its remarkable architectural landmarks and vibrant atmosphere make it a must-visit destination for travelers. Begin your exploration at the awe-inspiring Seville Cathedral, the largest Gothic cathedral in the world, which houses the tomb of Christopher Columbus. Climb the Giralda Tower for panoramic views of the city, offering a breathtaking vista that stretches to the horizon.

Next, venture into the Alcazar palace, a stunning complex that showcases a fusion of Moorish and Mudéjar architectural styles. Stroll through the enchanting gardens adorned with fountains, orange trees, and colorful tiles, and immerse yourself in the serenity of this royal residence.

Seville's rich culinary scene is another highlight not to be missed. Indulge in a tapeo, a tradition of hopping from one tapas bar to another, savoring delectable bites and experiencing the lively atmosphere. The Triana neighborhood, known for its flamenco heritage, offers an authentic and vibrant experience of this passionate art form.

In addition to these three remarkable destinations, Andalucia is also home to many other cities and landmarks that offer their own unique charms. From the picturesque white-washed villages of Ronda and Mijas to the historic city of Cadiz with its stunning coastline, the region is a treasure trove of cultural and architectural gems waiting to be discovered.

Here are more iconic landmarks and must-visit cities in Andalucia that deserve to be on your itinerary:

The Alcazaba of Malaga:

Situated in the heart of Malaga, the Alcazaba stands as a formidable testament to the region's Moorish heritage. This impressive fortress, dating back to the 11th century, offers visitors a glimpse into the rich history of Andalucia. As you explore its labyrinthine passages, picturesque gardens, and intricate courtyards, you'll be transported back in time to an era of Islamic splendor.

Climbing to the top of the Alcazaba rewards you with breathtaking panoramic views of Malaga and the glistening Mediterranean Sea. Take in the sight of the city's skyline, with its blend of ancient and modern architecture, and admire the surrounding landscapes that stretch as far as the eye can see.

The Roman Bridge of Cordoba:

Crossing the Guadalquivir River in Cordoba, the Roman Bridge is an architectural marvel that dates back to the 1st century BC. It stands as a testament to the city's ancient Roman roots and connects the historic center of Cordoba with the modern district. As you stroll across the bridge, you'll be enveloped in a sense of history, imagining the countless feet that have traversed this ancient path over the centuries.

The Roman Bridge offers captivating views of the city's skyline, including the iconic Mezquita and the Alcazar. As the sun sets, the bridge becomes bathed in a warm glow, creating a picturesque setting for a leisurely stroll or a moment of quiet contemplation.

The Plaza de España in Seville:

Prepare to be mesmerized by the grandeur of the Plaza de España, an architectural masterpiece nestled within Seville's Maria Luisa Park. This vast square, built in 1928 for the Ibero-American Exposition, is a perfect example of Spanish Renaissance Revival architecture, combining elements of Moorish and Renaissance styles.

As you wander through the plaza, you'll be captivated by the beauty of its tiled alcoves, elaborately decorated fountains, and a charming canal that winds its way through the square. Each alcove represents a different province of Spain, showcasing intricate ceramic tilework that depicts historical scenes and motifs. Rent a rowboat and glide along the canal, taking in the serenity of the surroundings and admiring the architectural splendor that surrounds you.

The Giralda Tower in Seville:

One of the most iconic landmarks in Seville, the Giralda Tower is an emblem of the city's rich history and cultural heritage. Originally built as a minaret for the Great Mosque of Seville, it later became the bell tower of the Seville Cathedral.

Ascend the tower via its gently sloping ramps, which were designed to allow horses to reach the top. As you make your way up, marvel at the intricate brickwork and Islamic architectural details that have stood the test of time. Upon reaching the summit, be rewarded with breathtaking panoramic views of Seville's cityscape, including the cathedral itself, the Plaza de España, and the picturesque neighborhoods that make up the city.

The Royal Alcazar of Seville:

Prepare to be transported to a world of enchantment as you step into the Royal Alcazar of Seville. This stunning palace complex, with its lush gardens, elaborate tilework, and an exquisite blend of architectural styles, is a true gem of Andalucia.

The Alcazar showcases the region's rich history, reflecting the influences of the Moors, Christians, and Renaissance artisans who contributed to its construction and design. As you wander through its halls and courtyards, adorned with intricate carvings, colorful tiles, and serene water features, you'll feel like you've stepped into a fairy tale. Don't miss the enchanting Gardens of the Alcazar, with their meticulously landscaped paths, hidden nooks, and fragrant orange trees.

The Caminito del Rey:

For the adventurous souls seeking a thrilling experience amidst nature, the Caminito del Rey is an absolute must. This narrow pathway clings to the steep cliffs of El Chorro Gorge, offering breathtaking views of the natural landscape that surrounds you.

Originally constructed as a service walkway for workers maintaining a nearby hydroelectric power plant, the Caminito del Rey has gained fame as a thrilling hiking trail. Traverse the suspended walkways, suspended over the rugged terrain, and marvel at the stunning rock formations, deep gorges, and cascading waterfalls that make this place truly extraordinary.

As you navigate the trail, take the time to appreciate the magnitude of human engineering and the harmonious coexistence between mankind and nature in this awe-inspiring setting.

The Puente Nuevo in Ronda:

Ronda, perched dramatically on a deep gorge, is home to the iconic Puente Nuevo, or "New Bridge." Spanning the Tajo Gorge, this architectural marvel offers not only a means of crossing between Ronda's old and new towns but also awe-inspiring panoramic vistas of the surrounding countryside.

As you make your way across the bridge, take in the breathtaking views of the El Tajo Gorge, where the Guadalevín River flows hundreds of feet below. Admire the architectural mastery that went into the bridge's construction, standing as a testament to Ronda's engineering prowess. For the most unforgettable experience, visit during sunset, when the warm light bathes the landscape, casting a magical glow over the surroundings.

The Cathedral of Cadiz:

Dominating the skyline of Cadiz, the Cathedral of Cadiz is a magnificent example of Baroque architecture. With its golden dome and intricate details, this grand cathedral is not only a place of worship but also a symbol of the city's rich history.

Step inside and marvel at the opulent interior, adorned with ornate altarpieces, majestic columns, and stunning works of art. Climb to the top of the bell tower for sweeping views of Cadiz, including its historic neighborhoods, golden beaches, and the shimmering Atlantic Ocean.

The White Villages of Andalucia:

Andalucia is renowned for its picturesque white villages, nestled amidst stunning natural landscapes. These charming towns, with their whitewashed facades and narrow cobblestone streets, offer a glimpse into traditional Andalusian life and provide a tranquil retreat from the bustling cities.

Among the white villages worth exploring are Zahara de la Sierra, with its medieval castle and breathtaking views of the Sierra de Grazalema; Setenil de las Bodegas, where houses are built into the cliffs, creating a unique architectural spectacle; and Frigiliana, renowned for its Moorish charm, colorful flower-filled streets, and panoramic views of the Mediterranean Sea.

The Mezquita de las Tornerías in Toledo:

While not located within Andalucia, the Mezquita de las Tornerías in Toledo is an exceptional example of Moorish architecture and provides a fascinating glimpse into the cultural interplay between Moorish and Christian influences.

This mosque-turned-church showcases the rich history and architectural heritage of Toledo. Explore its horseshoe arches, intricate tilework, and serene prayer halls, which transport you back to the time when the city flourished under Moorish rule. Witness the blending of styles as Christian elements were incorporated into the mosque after the Reconquista, creating a remarkable fusion of cultures and architectural forms.

The Baelo Claudia Ruins in Tarifa:

Travel back in time as you explore the well-preserved Baelo Claudia Ruins in Tarifa. This ancient Roman city was once a bustling trading hub and offers a fascinating glimpse into the region's ancient history.

Wander through the ruins and envision the city's former grandeur. Marvel at the well-preserved amphitheater, where gladiators once fought for the entertainment of the crowds. Explore the remains of the temples, forums, and marketplace, where merchants from across the Roman Empire once gathered to trade goods and ideas.

As you roam the site, you'll gain insights into the daily life of the ancient Romans, appreciating their architectural achievements and their cultural and economic influence in the region. Take a moment to imagine the vibrant community that once thrived in this coastal city, which overlooked the Strait of Gibraltar and served as a vital gateway between Europe and Africa.

Visiting the Baelo Claudia Ruins is like stepping into a time capsule, transporting you back to a bygone era and giving you a deeper appreciation for the enduring legacies of civilizations that have shaped Andalucia.As you embark on your journey through Andalucia, be prepared to be enthralled by the architectural wonders of the Alhambra, the Mezquita, and the captivating city of Seville. These icons of Andalucia represent the region's historical and cultural legacy, offering a glimpse into its glorious past and vibrant present. So, wander through the centuries, marvel at the intricate details, and let the enchanting landmarks and cities of Andalucia leave an indelible impression on your soul.

Practical Tips for Traveling in Andalucia

When it comes to traveling in Andalucia, a little preparation and insider knowledge can go a long way. This section provides you with a comprehensive guide to ensure a smooth and enjoyable experience as you explore the wonders of Southern Spain. From transportation and accommodation to local customs and safety considerations, these practical tips will help you make the most of your time in Andalucia.

Best Time to Visit:

Andalucia's Mediterranean climate is one of its most appealing features, attracting visitors year-round. With hot summers and mild winters, the region offers a pleasant and inviting atmosphere for travelers seeking a diverse range of experiences. When planning your visit to Andalucia, understanding the climate and considering your preferences and desired activities will help you determine the best time to explore this captivating region.

The spring months of April to June are particularly delightful in Andalucia. The temperatures are comfortably warm, ranging from the mid-60s to low 80s Fahrenheit (around 15-28 degrees Celsius). The countryside is in full bloom, with colorful flowers carpeting the landscapes, creating a picturesque backdrop for your adventures. It is a great time for outdoor activities such as hiking, sightseeing, and exploring the region's natural wonders.

In addition to the pleasant weather, the spring months in Andalucia are known for vibrant festivals and celebrations. Semana Santa, or Holy Week, is a significant religious event that takes place in cities throughout the region. It is a time when streets come alive with processions of elaborately adorned religious floats, accompanied by solemn music and passionate expressions of faith. If you have an interest in experiencing this unique cultural event, planning your visit during Semana Santa will provide an immersive and unforgettable experience.

Another notable festival that occurs in the spring is the Feria de Abril in Seville. Held two weeks after Semana Santa, the Feria is a week-long extravaganza of flamenco dancing, bullfighting, horse parades, and lively street parties. The entire city is transformed into a colorful spectacle with beautifully decorated marquees (casetas) lining the fairground. Attending the Feria de Abril allows you to witness the exuberance and joie de vivre that characterizes Andalusian culture.

If you prefer milder temperatures and fewer crowds, the fall months of September to October are an excellent time to visit Andalucia. With average temperatures ranging from the mid-70s to mid-80s Fahrenheit (around 20-30 degrees Celsius), the weather remains pleasant, and the summer heat starts to dissipate. It's an ideal period for exploring Andalucia's cities, cultural sites, and coastal areas without feeling overwhelmed by high temperatures or large tourist crowds.

During the fall, you can also witness the grape harvest and participate in wine-related activities in the region's renowned vineyards. The harvest season brings a festive atmosphere to wineries, offering the opportunity to learn about Andalucia's winemaking traditions and taste some of its acclaimed wines.

It's worth noting that Andalucia's coastal regions, including the Costa del Sol and Costa de la Luz, are popular summer destinations. If you enjoy beach activities, swimming, and sunbathing, the summer months from June to August offer the warmest water temperatures and a lively beach scene. However, be prepared for larger crowds and higher accommodation prices during this peak tourist season.

Ultimately, the best time to visit Andalucia depends on your personal preferences and the experiences you seek. Whether you're captivated by cultural events, interested in outdoor adventures, or simply want to savor the region's rich history and cuisine, Andalucia offers something special year-round. By considering the climate, festivals, and crowd levels, you can choose the ideal time to immerse yourself in the wonders of this diverse and enchanting region of Southern Spain.

Transportation:

Getting around Andalucia is a breeze, thanks to its efficient and well-connected transportation network. Whether you're arriving by air or planning to explore the region's cities, towns, and countryside, there are various transportation options available to suit your needs and preferences.

International Airports:

Andalucia is served by several international airports, making it easily accessible for travelers from around the world. The major airports in the region include Seville Airport, Malaga Airport, and Granada Airport. These airports offer numerous flights to and from domestic and international destinations, providing convenient entry points for your Andalusian adventure.

Upon arrival, you'll find a range of transportation options to take you from the airports to your desired destinations. Taxis and private transfers are readily available and provide a convenient and hassle-free way to reach your accommodation. Many hotels also offer shuttle services for their guests. Additionally, car rental companies have counters at the airports, allowing you to rent a vehicle for greater flexibility during your stay.

High-Speed Train (AVE):

Andalucia is well-connected by the high-speed train network known as the AVE (Alta Velocidad Española). The AVE provides fast and comfortable travel between major cities, allowing you to cover long distances efficiently. The primary AVE stations in Andalucia are located in Seville, Malaga, and

Cordoba, with connections to other Spanish cities such as Madrid and Barcelona.

Traveling by AVE offers a seamless experience with modern amenities and convenient schedules. The trains are spacious and equipped with comfortable seating, power outlets, and onboard services. With high speeds reaching up to 300 km/h (186 mph), you can swiftly journey between cities and make the most of your time in Andalucia.

Local Trains:

In addition to the AVE, Andalucia has an extensive local train network that connects cities, towns, and rural areas. Renfe is the national train company in Spain, and its local trains (Cercanías) are an excellent option for exploring the region at a more relaxed pace. The local trains are comfortable, affordable, and offer scenic views as they traverse the picturesque Andalusian landscapes.

These trains are ideal for day trips to nearby destinations, such as Ronda from Malaga or Cadiz from Seville. They provide a convenient means of transportation, allowing you to discover the charming towns, coastal delights, and natural wonders that lie beyond the major cities.

Buses:

Buses are a popular mode of transportation in Andalucia, offering extensive coverage and connectivity across the region. The bus network is well-developed, making it an affordable and convenient option for both short and long-distance travel.

Local buses are available within cities and towns, providing easy access to various neighborhoods and attractions. They offer a cost-effective way to explore urban areas and reach specific points of interest. Intercity buses connect different cities and towns, offering an extensive network that reaches even the smallest Andalusian villages.

Several bus companies operate in Andalucia, including ALSA, Avanza, and Socibus. These companies provide reliable services, comfortable seating, and air-conditioned coaches, ensuring a pleasant journey. Tickets can be purchased at bus stations, online, or directly from the driver, depending on the company and route.

Taxis and Ridesharing:

Taxis are readily available throughout Andalucia, offering a convenient and flexible means of transportation, especially for short trips or when exploring areas not well-served by public transportation. Taxi ranks can be found in city centers, near tourist attractions, and at transportation hubs like airports and train stations.

In recent years, ridesharing services such as Uber and Cabify have also become increasingly popular in major Andalusian cities like Seville, Malaga, and Granada. These services provide an alternative to traditional taxis, allowing you to easily book a ride using a smartphone app.

Driving:

Renting a car is an excellent option if you prefer the freedom and flexibility to explore Andalucia at your own pace. Having a car gives you the opportunity to venture off the beaten path, reach remote areas, and discover hidden gems that may not be easily accessible by public transportation.

The road infrastructure in Andalucia is well-maintained, with modern highways connecting major cities and towns. However, it's worth noting that driving in city centers can be challenging due to narrow streets, one-way systems, and limited parking options. It's advisable to familiarize yourself with local traffic rules, parking regulations, and driving customs before embarking on your journey.

Gas stations are plentiful along major routes, and you'll find both full-service and self-service options. Make sure to have a valid driver's license and insurance coverage, and consider renting a GPS or using smartphone navigation apps for easy navigation.

In conclusion, getting around Andalucia is a breeze thanks to its excellent transportation infrastructure. From international airports to high-speed trains, buses, taxis, and rental cars, you have a plethora of options to choose from. Whether you're exploring the region's vibrant cities, picturesque towns, or enchanting countryside, these transportation choices ensure that you can navigate Andalucia with ease and make the most of your unforgettable journey through Southern Spain.

Accommodation:

Andalucia, with its diverse landscapes and vibrant cities, provides a plethora of accommodation options to cater to every traveler's preferences and budget. Whether you're seeking luxury, charm, or budget-friendly stays, the region has something for everyone. From traditional Andalusian houses to rural cortijos (country houses), the accommodation choices in Andalucia offer a chance to immerse yourself in the local culture and experience the region's unique charm.

Luxury Hotels:

When it comes to luxury accommodations, Andalucia sets the stage for an indulgent and unforgettable experience. In cities like Seville, Granada, and Marbella, you'll find a selection of prestigious hotels that offer world-class amenities and impeccable service. These luxurious properties combine elegance, sophistication, and modern comforts to create an oasis of opulence.

Step into the grand lobby of a luxury hotel, where you'll be greeted by polished marble floors, exquisite chandeliers, and tasteful artwork. The well-appointed rooms and suites boast plush furnishings, sumptuous bedding, and stunning views of the cityscape or the Mediterranean Sea. High-end amenities such as spa facilities, swimming pools, and fitness centers cater to your relaxation and wellness needs.

Fine dining is an integral part of the luxury hotel experience in Andalucia. Indulge in gourmet cuisine prepared by talented chefs who blend traditional Andalusian flavors with innovative techniques. From Michelin-starred restaurants to rooftop bars with panoramic views, these establishments offer a culinary journey that tantalizes the taste buds.

Cozy Guesthouses:

For a more intimate and personalized experience, consider staying in a cozy guesthouse or a boutique hotel. Andalucia is known for its charming guesthouses, often housed in converted historic buildings or traditional Andalusian houses. These accommodations provide a unique ambiance and a sense of authenticity that transports you back in time.

Each guesthouse has its own character and charm, with tastefully decorated rooms that reflect the region's heritage. Expect exposed wooden beams, handcrafted furniture, and locally sourced artwork that add to the ambiance. Many guesthouses also offer communal areas such as lounges or courtyards, where guests can relax, read a book, or enjoy a cup of traditional Spanish coffee.

What sets guesthouses apart is the personalized service and attention to detail. The friendly and attentive staff often goes the extra mile to ensure your comfort and satisfaction. They are knowledgeable about the local area and can provide insider tips on the best restaurants, hidden gems, and off-the-beaten-path attractions.

Budget-Friendly Hostels:

If you're traveling on a budget or seeking a social atmosphere, Andalucia's hostels are an excellent option. Hostels in cities like Seville, Malaga, and Cadiz offer affordable dormitory-style rooms with shared facilities, as well as private rooms for those who prefer more privacy. Many hostels also have communal spaces such as lounges, kitchens, and outdoor terraces, where travelers can connect, socialize, and exchange travel stories.

Staying in a hostel not only saves you money but also provides an opportunity to meet fellow travelers from around the world. Share tips and recommendations, join group activities organized by the hostel, or simply enjoy the vibrant atmosphere created by like-minded individuals. Hostels are known for their friendly and laid-back ambiance, making them ideal for solo travelers or those looking to make new friends.

Traditional Andalusian Houses:

For an authentic and immersive experience, staying in a traditional Andalusian house, known as a casa rural or casa de campo, is highly recommended. These houses are often located in the countryside or picturesque villages, allowing you to escape the hustle and bustle of the city and embrace the tranquility of rural Andalucia.

Traditional Andalusian houses are typically whitewashed structures adorned with colorful tiles, wooden balconies, and vibrant flowers. They feature rustic interiors with thick stone walls, tiled floors, and traditional furnishings. Many houses have courtyards or gardens where you can relax, read a book, or enjoy a meal surrounded by fragrant orange trees or blooming bougainvillea.

One of the highlights of staying in a traditional Andalusian house is the opportunity to savor homemade meals prepared by the hosts. The cuisine often showcases local flavors and traditional recipes, giving you a taste of authentic Andalusian gastronomy. Engage in conversations with the hosts, learn about their way of life, and gain insights into the local culture and traditions.

Rural Cortijos:

Andalucia's rural cortijos, or country houses, offer a unique blend of rustic charm, tranquility, and modern comforts. These properties, often located amidst olive groves, vineyards, or rolling hills, provide a serene and idyllic setting for a relaxing getaway. Cortijos range from small family-run establishments to larger properties with luxurious amenities.

Step into a rural cortijo, and you'll be greeted by spacious rooms adorned with traditional décor and modern amenities. Enjoy the cozy atmosphere created by wooden beams, stone walls, and antique furniture. Many cortijos also offer outdoor spaces such as gardens, patios, or swimming pools, where you can unwind and soak in the breathtaking natural surroundings.

Rural cortijos provide an excellent opportunity to connect with nature and experience the beauty of the Andalusian countryside. Take leisurely walks through the olive groves, go horseback riding in the rolling hills, or simply relax in a hammock with a book. The peacefulness and tranquility of the rural setting offer a welcome respite from the bustling city life.

Booking in Advance:

In popular cities like Seville, Granada, and Malaga, it's advisable to book your accommodation in advance, especially during peak seasons. These cities attract a significant number of tourists throughout the year, and securing your preferred accommodation ensures that you have a wide range of options and can secure the best rates.

Booking in advance also allows you to choose accommodations in prime locations, whether it's a luxury hotel with stunning views, a guesthouse in the heart of the historic district, or a hostel close to popular attractions. By planning ahead, you can avoid last-minute stress and have peace of mind knowing that your accommodation is secured.

Additionally, if you plan to visit Andalucia during popular festivals or events, such as Semana Santa or the Feria de Abril, early booking is essential. These celebrations attract a large influx of visitors, and accommodations in central locations tend to fill up quickly.

Alternative Accommodation:

In addition to traditional hotels, guesthouses, and hostels, Andalucia offers unique and alternative accommodation options for those seeking something out of the ordinary. Consider staying in a rural farmhouse (finca), an eco-friendly lodge, or a glamping site to immerse yourself in nature and experience a different side of Andalucia.

Rural farmhouses, or fincas, are ideal for nature lovers and those seeking a peaceful retreat in the countryside. These properties often offer comfortable accommodations surrounded by expansive farmland or vineyards. Wake up to the sounds of birds chirping, take leisurely walks through the fields, and enjoy farm-to-table meals prepared with fresh local produce.

Eco-friendly lodges provide an opportunity to stay in harmony with nature while minimizing your ecological footprint. These sustainable accommodations are designed with environmentally friendly practices in mind, such as using renewable energy, minimizing waste, and promoting eco-tourism initiatives. Staying in an eco-lodge allows you to enjoy nature while being conscious of your impact on the environment.

For a unique and adventurous experience, consider glamping in Andalucia. Glamping sites offer luxurious tents or accommodations with all the comforts of a hotel, including comfortable beds, private bathrooms, and sometimes even private hot tubs. Wake up to breathtaking views, stargaze at night, and experience the beauty of nature while enjoying the amenities of a hotel.

Local Recommendations:

To enhance your stay in Andalucia and discover hidden gems, don't hesitate to seek recommendations fromthe locals. The friendly Andalusians are often more than willing to share their favorite places to stay and lesser-known accommodations that may not be widely known to tourists. Engaging in conversations with locals, such as restaurant owners, tour guides, or shopkeepers, can provide valuable insights into unique and off-the-beaten-path accommodations.

These recommendations can lead you to hidden boutique hotels tucked away in narrow streets, family-run guesthouses with exceptional hospitality, or charming bed and breakfasts with a personal touch. Locals can also provide insider tips on nearby attractions, local markets, and authentic restaurants that are off the tourist radar.

When seeking local recommendations, be open to trying new experiences and venturing beyond the usual tourist spots.

Whether it's a small family-owned guesthouse in a remote village or a charming bed and breakfast nestled in the mountains, these hidden accommodations can offer a more intimate and immersive experience, allowing you to connect with the local culture and lifestyle.

When it comes to finding and booking accommodation in Andalucia, several popular apps and websites can help you discover the best options based on your preferences and budget. Here are some well-known platforms that are commonly used for booking accommodations in Andalucia:

Booking.com: Booking.com is one of the most widely used platforms for finding and booking accommodations worldwide, including Andalucia. It offers a wide range of options, from luxury hotels to budget-friendly guesthouses and apartments. The platform provides user reviews, detailed property descriptions, and convenient search filters to help you find the perfect accommodation for your needs.

Airbnb: Airbnb is a popular online marketplace that connects travelers with hosts who offer unique accommodations, such as private rooms, apartments, or entire houses. In Andalucia, you can find a variety of options, including traditional Andalusian houses, apartments with stunning views, and cozy guesthouses. Airbnb allows you to communicate directly with hosts and provides a secure platform for booking and payment.

Expedia: Expedia is a well-known travel booking platform that offers a wide selection of accommodations, including hotels, vacation rentals, and all-inclusive resorts. With its extensive inventory, Expedia provides a range of options in Andalucia, allowing you to compare prices, read reviews, and book your preferred accommodation.

Hotels.com: Hotels.com is another popular platform that specializes in hotel bookings. It offers a vast selection of hotels in Andalucia, ranging from budget options to luxury establishments. Hotels.com provides detailed property information, customer reviews, and a loyalty program that rewards frequent travelers with free stays.

HomeAway: HomeAway is a vacation rental marketplace owned by Expedia Group. It offers a wide range of vacation rentals, including private villas, apartments, and cottages. HomeAway allows you to search for accommodations in Andalucia based on specific criteria, such as amenities, location, and property type, providing a diverse selection for your stay.

TripAdvisor: TripAdvisor is a popular travel platform that not only offers reviews and recommendations but also allows you to book accommodations directly through its platform. It provides a comprehensive list of hotels, vacation rentals, and B&Bs in Andalucia, along with traveler reviews, ratings, and photos to help you make informed decisions.

Hostelworld: If you're looking for budget-friendly options or hostels in Andalucia, Hostelworld is a go-to platform. It specializes in hostel bookings and offers a wide selection of dormitory rooms, private rooms, and social spaces. Hostelworld provides detailed descriptions, photos, and user reviews to help you choose the right hostel for your needs.

It's worth noting that availability and pricing may vary across different platforms, so it's recommended to compare prices and read reviews before making a booking. Additionally, some accommodations in Andalucia might not be listed on all platforms, so exploring multiple sources can increase your chances of finding unique and off-the-beaten-path options.

Remember to check the cancellation policies, payment methods, and any additional fees before finalizing your booking. By utilizing these popular apps and websites, you can easily find and secure the perfect accommodation for your stay in Andalucia, ensuring a comfortable and enjoyable travel experience.

In conclusion, Andalucia offers a diverse range of accommodation options that cater to every traveler's needs and preferences. From luxury hotels to cozy guesthouses, budget-friendly hostels to traditional Andalusian houses and rural cortijos, the region ensures there's a perfect place for you to rest and rejuvenate during your exploration of Southern Spain. Embrace the charm and hospitality of Andalucia, and let your accommodation choice enhance your overall travel experience.

Local Customs and Etiquette:

Andalucia, with its warm and welcoming culture, offers visitors an opportunity to connect with the locals on a personal level. By understanding and embracing a few local customs and etiquette, you can enhance your interactions and create memorable experiences during your time in this vibrant region of Southern Spain.

Greetings in Andalucia are typically warm and friendly, reflecting the hospitable nature of the people. Handshakes are common when meeting someone for the first time, but as you become more familiar, cheek kisses are often exchanged. It is customary to greet others with a smile and maintain eye contact during conversations, as this demonstrates respect and engagement.

Spaniards, including Andalusians, tend to have a relaxed approach to time. Schedules and appointments are often seen as flexible, and punctuality may not be as rigid as in some other cultures. It is advisable to adopt a similar mindset and not be overly concerned if plans deviate slightly from the original schedule. Embracing this relaxed attitude will allow you to immerse yourself in the unhurried pace of Andalusian life and fully appreciate the experience.

When dining out in Andalucia, it is customary to greet the staff and fellow diners with a friendly "Hola" (hello) or "Buenas tardes" (good afternoon) upon entering a restaurant. This simple gesture sets a positive tone and shows respect for the establishment and those around you. Andalusians are known for their love of good food and take pride in their cuisine, so be sure to indulge in the local specialties.

Andalucian cuisine is a delightful blend of flavors and influences from its diverse history. Don't miss the opportunity to savor traditional dishes such as gazpacho, a refreshing cold soup made with tomatoes, cucumbers, and other fresh ingredients. Paella, a rice-based dish typically featuring a combination of seafood, meat, and vegetables, is another must-try delicacy. And of course, no visit to Andalucia would be complete without sampling tapas, which are small plates of various savory dishes meant for sharing. Tapas culture is deeply ingrained in Andalusian life, and enjoying these flavorful bites with a glass of local wine or a refreshing sangria is a quintessential Andalusian experience.

When it comes to tipping in Andalucia, it is appreciated but not obligatory. Service charges are often included in the bill, especially in tourist areas. However, leaving a small amount of change or rounding up the bill is considered polite and a gesture of appreciation for good service. If you receive exceptional service or wish to show additional gratitude, a slightly higher tip is always welcome.

Throughout Andalucia, you'll find a plethora of restaurants, from casual tapas bars to fine dining establishments. Don't hesitate to ask the waitstaff for recommendations or guidance in selecting dishes. They are often knowledgeable about local specialties and can offer suggestions based on your preferences.

Beyond the dining experience, Andalucians are known for their warmth and friendliness. Engaging in conversations with locals is a great way to immerse yourself in the culture and gain insights into their way of life. Even if your Spanish language skills are limited, making an effort to learn a few basic phrases and greetings will be appreciated and can help break the ice.

By embracing the customs and etiquette of Andalucia, you will forge connections with the locals and create memorable interactions. The warmth and welcoming nature of the Andalusian people, combined with the delectable cuisine, will ensure that your journey through this captivating region leaves a lasting impression. So, dive into the culinary delights, exchange friendly greetings, and embrace the relaxed pace of life as you explore the treasures of Andalucia.

Safety Considerations:

Andalucia is known for its warm hospitality and friendly atmosphere, making it a generally safe destination for travelers. However, it's always important to exercise caution and take necessary precautions to ensure a trouble-free journey. Here are some practical tips to help you stay safe while exploring this beautiful region.

Keeping Your Belongings Secure:

Like in any tourist destination, it's crucial to keep your belongings secure to avoid falling victim to pickpocketing or theft. Be mindful of your surroundings, especially in crowded areas, markets, and tourist attractions where thieves may take advantage of distractions.

Consider using a money belt or a secure bag to carry your valuables, such as your passport, cash, and important documents. Keep a close eye on your belongings at all times and avoid displaying expensive items unnecessarily. Be cautious with your mobile devices and cameras, especially in busy public transportation or crowded streets.

Driving and Traffic Safety:

If you plan to rent a car and explore the countryside of Andalucia, it's important to familiarize yourself with the local traffic rules and regulations. Spain drives on the right-hand side of the road, and speed limits and traffic signs must be obeyed.

In cities, pay attention to parking restrictions and be aware of designated parking areas to avoid fines or towing. It's advisable to park in secure and well-lit areas. Avoid leaving any valuable items visible inside the car, as car break-ins can occur in popular tourist areas.

When driving on narrow and winding roads, especially in rural areas or mountainous regions, exercise caution and be prepared for unexpected turns and oncoming traffic. Take your time, follow the speed limits, and stay focused on the road. If you're not comfortable driving in unfamiliar terrain, consider hiring a local driver or relying on public transportation.

Travel Insurance:

Having comprehensive travel insurance is essential when visiting Andalucia or any other destination. Ensure that your travel insurance covers medical emergencies, including hospitalization and emergency medical evacuation if needed. It's also important to have coverage for trip cancellations, lost baggage, and personal liability.

Before purchasing travel insurance, carefully read the policy to understand the coverage limits and exclusions. If you plan on participating in adventure activities or renting a car, make sure your insurance covers these activities as well.

Emergency Contacts and Local Assistance:

Before your trip, make note of emergency contact numbers, including the local police (112), medical services, and your embassy or consulate's contact information. Keep these numbers easily accessible, either on your phone or in a physical notebook.

In case of any emergency or if you require assistance, reach out to the local authorities or your embassy/consulate for guidance. They can provide valuable support and information in times of need.

Cultural Sensitivity:

Respecting the local culture and customs is important while traveling in Andalucia. The Andalusian people are generally warm and welcoming, and by showing appreciation for their traditions, you can have a more positive experience.

Dress appropriately, especially when visiting religious sites or attending formal events. It's advisable to cover your shoulders and avoid wearing revealing clothing out of respect for local customs. Learning a few basic Spanish phrases can also help in your interactions and show a genuine interest in the local culture.

Staying Informed:

Stay updated on local news and travel advisories before and during your trip to Andalucia. It's recommended to check the website or contact the consulate or embassy of your home country for any travel advisories or safety alerts related to Andalucia.

Additionally, consider registering your travel plans with your embassy or consulate through their online registration systems. This enables them to contact you and provide assistance in case of emergencies or unforeseen circumstances.

By following these practical tips, you can ensure a safe and enjoyable experience while traveling in Andalucia. By staying vigilant, respecting local customs, and taking necessary precautions, you can focus on immersing yourself in the rich culture, stunning landscapes, and vibrant atmosphere that this region has to offer. Remember to embrace the spirit of adventure while prioritizing your safety and well-being throughout your journey.

Language:

Spanish is the official language of Andalucia, as it is in the rest of Spain. While many people in tourist areas and establishments speak English, making an effort to learn a few basic Spanish phrases can greatly enhance your travel experience. It shows respect for the local culture and opens doors to deeper connections with the people you meet along the way.

Even if your Spanish skills are limited, knowing a few key phrases can go a long way. Simple greetings like "Hola" (hello) and "Gracias" (thank you) are always appreciated and can create a positive impression. When entering a shop or restaurant, a friendly "Buenos días" (good morning), "Buenas tardes" (good afternoon), or "Buenas noches" (good evening/night) sets a polite tone and establishes a connection.

Learning basic phrases for ordering food, asking for directions, and engaging in simple conversations can also prove invaluable. Phrases such as "Una mesa para dos, por favor" (A table for two, please), "¿Dónde está el baño?" (Where is the bathroom?), or "¿Podría ayudarme?" (Could you help me?) can help you navigate daily situations with ease.

Locals in Andalucia are generally friendly and appreciative of visitors who make an effort to communicate in their language. They often respond warmly and enthusiastically, which can lead to more authentic interactions and memorable experiences. In small towns and villages where English proficiency might be limited, speaking even a few basic Spanish phrases can make a significant difference in your ability to connect with locals and gain insights into their culture.

Furthermore, learning some Spanish can be practical and beneficial when exploring off-the-beaten-path destinations or interacting with locals who may not be fluent in English. It can help you navigate local markets, negotiate prices, and seek recommendations for hidden gems that may not be on the typical tourist radar. Being able to engage in basic conversations allows you to form connections, ask for advice, and create a more immersive travel experience.

Fortunately, there are various resources available to help you learn Spanish, ranging from language learning apps and websites to phrasebooks and language classes. Taking the time to study basic vocabulary and practice pronunciation before your trip will boost your confidence and show locals that you value their language and culture.

Remember, the goal is not fluency but rather making an effort and showing respect. Even if you stumble over words or make mistakes, locals will appreciate your willingness to learn and engage with their language. They may even offer assistance, corrections, or further explanations to help you improve.

In conclusion, while English is spoken in tourist areas and establishments in Andalucia, making an effort to learn a few basic Spanish phrases can greatly enrich your travel experience. It demonstrates respect for the local culture, opens doors to deeper connections, and allows you to navigate daily situations more smoothly. So, embrace the opportunity to learn a new language, and don't be afraid to engage with the people of Andalucia in their mother tongue. Your efforts will be met with warmth and appreciation, making your journey through Southern Spain even more fulfilling.

Local Events and Festivals:

Andalucia, the land of flamenco, bullfighting, and rich cultural traditions, is widely acclaimed for its vibrant festivals and cultural events. These celebrations are deeply rooted in the region's history and offer a captivating glimpse into the Andalusian way of life. Two notable festivals that attract both locals and tourists alike are Semana Santa (Holy Week) and the Feria de Abril in Seville.

Semana Santa is one of the most significant religious events in Andalucia, commemorating the passion, death, and resurrection of Jesus Christ. This week-long celebration takes place in cities across the region, including Seville, Malaga, Granada, Cordoba, and Cadiz. The streets come alive with elaborate processions, religious statues, and penitents dressed in traditional robes.

Each procession is organized by a brotherhood (hermandad) and typically consists of pasos, which are richly adorned floats depicting scenes from the Passion of Christ or the Virgin Mary. These pasos are carried through the streets by costaleros, who bear the weight of the float on their shoulders. The processions are accompanied by solemn music played by brass bands and saetas (religious songs).

The atmosphere during Semana Santa is one of reverence and devotion, as thousands of locals and visitors gather to witness this extraordinary display of faith and artistic expression. It's a unique opportunity to experience the religious fervor and cultural heritage of Andalucia.

Another grand celebration in Andalucia is the Feria de Abril, held in Seville. This week-long extravaganza takes place two weeks after Semana Santa and marks the beginning of the festive season. The fairgrounds, known as the Real de la Feria, come alive with colorful casetas (marquees) where people gather to eat, drink, dance, and socialize.

The Feria de Abril is a joyful celebration of Andalusian culture, featuring flamenco performances, bullfights, equestrian shows, and lively street parties. The women don their traditional flamenco dresses (trajes de flamenca), adorned with ruffles, vibrant colors, and intricate designs, while men dress in suits or traditional attire.

Inside the casetas, you can immerse yourself in the Andalusian spirit as locals and visitors indulge in tapas, traditional dishes, and local wines. Flamenco music and dancing fill the air, creating a festive atmosphere that is truly unforgettable.

It's worth noting that Andalucia has numerous other festivals and events throughout the year, showcasing the region's cultural diversity and traditions. From the Carnival celebrations in Cadiz to the Patio Festival in Cordoba, each event offers a unique experience and a chance to engage with the local community.

Before planning your trip to Andalucia, it is highly recommended to check the local event calendars to see if there are any festivals or events happening during your visit. These celebrations provide an authentic and immersive experience, allowing you to witness the vibrant spirit, artistic expressions, and deep-rooted traditions of Andalusian culture.

Attending these festivals and cultural events requires some preparation. It's advisable to book accommodations well in advance, as they tend to fill up quickly during these peak times. Familiarize yourself with the festival schedules, procession routes, and other relevant information to make the most of your experience.

Additionally, it's a good idea to embrace the local customs and traditions during these festivals. Try learning a few flamenco dance steps or basic phrases in Spanish to interact with the locals and join in the festivities. Respect the religious and cultural significance of the events, and be mindful of the dress code if there are any specific guidelines.

Participating in Andalucia's vibrant festivals and cultural events is an incredible opportunity to immerse yourself in the region's rich heritage and experience the lively spirit of its people. The combination of religious devotion, artistic performances, culinary delights, and joyful celebrations makes these festivals an integral part of the Andalusian identity. So, plan your visit accordingly, embrace the festivities, and create lifelong memories of your journey through the heart of Andalucia.

Exploring Off the Beaten Path:

While popular cities like Seville, Granada, and Cordoba undoubtedly hold immense charm and historical significance, the true essence of Andalucia can also be found in its lesser-known, off-the-beaten-path destinations. Venturing beyond the tourist hotspots allows you to uncover hidden gems and experience the authentic Andalusian way of life. Here are a few recommendations for exploring the enchanting white-washed villages and picturesque landscapes of Andalucia.

Ronda:

Perched dramatically atop a deep gorge, Ronda is an awe-inspiring town that captures the imagination with its stunning vistas and rich cultural heritage. As you arrive in Ronda, your eyes will be drawn to the iconic Puente Nuevo, an architectural masterpiece that spans the El Tajo canyon. Walk across the bridge and be rewarded with panoramic views of the rugged landscape below. Take a moment to appreciate the engineering feat and the sheer beauty of the surroundings.

Wandering through the narrow streets of the old town, you'll encounter a fascinating blend of Moorish and Spanish influences. Discover the 13th-century Arab Baths, a testament to Ronda's Moorish past and a glimpse into the region's historical bathing traditions. The baths, adorned with elegant arches and intricate tilework, offer a tranquil setting for reflection.

Another highlight of Ronda is the Plaza de Toros, one of the oldest bullrings in Spain. Step inside this historical arena, which has witnessed centuries of bullfighting tradition. Explore the museum within the bullring to gain insight into the cultural significance and controversy surrounding this traditional spectacle. Even if you are not a fan of bullfighting, the architectural grandeur of the arena itself is worth experiencing.

Vejer de la Frontera:

Located on a hilltop in the province of Cadiz, Vejer de la Frontera is a picturesque medieval village that enchants visitors with its timeless beauty. As you stroll through its labyrinthine streets, you'll be captivated by the charm of white-washed houses adorned with colorful flowers. The Moorish influence is evident in the architectural details, from the narrow alleys and hidden courtyards to the decorative tiles and arched doorways.

One of the highlights of Vejer de la Frontera is the 11th-century Castle of Vejer. Perched atop the hill, the castle offers commanding views of the surrounding countryside, including glimpses of the Atlantic Ocean in the distance. Take a leisurely walk along the castle walls, and let your imagination transport you back in time to the era of knights and medieval battles.

Food lovers will delight in the gastronomic delights of Vejer de la Frontera. The village is known for its exceptional seafood, with local specialties such as almadraba tuna and fried fish gracing the menus of its traditional taverns and upscale restaurants. Pair your meal with locally produced wines, as the region is also renowned for its viticulture. Indulge in a culinary journey through the flavors of Andalusia as you savor the freshness and quality of the local cuisine.

Frigiliana:

Nestled in the foothills of the Sierra de Almijara, the charming village of Frigiliana is a true gem of Andalucia. Its picturesque beauty and Moorish influence make it a must-visit destination for travelers seeking an authentic experience. As you explore the narrow cobbled streets, you'll be enchanted by the vibrant bursts of color from the flowers that adorn the whitewashed houses.

Immerse yourself in the village's rich history and culture by visiting the Church of San Antonio. Admire its striking Mudejar-style bell tower and step inside to appreciate the beautiful interior adorned with religious artwork. Wander through the handicraft shops, where you can find locally made ceramics, textiles, and jewelry. Be sure to sample the local honey, a specialty of the region known for its exquisite flavor.

If you're fortunate enough to visit Frigiliana during the summer months, you'll have the opportunity to witness the Festival of the Three Cultures. This annual event celebrates the village's rich Moorish heritage with music, dance, and traditional costumes. The streets come alive with vibrant performances, creating an atmosphere of joy and cultural unity.

Alpujarra:

A scenic drive through the Alpujarra region is a journey through terraced hillsides, charming white villages, and a captivating blend of Moorish and Andalusian traditions.

Pampaneira, Bubión, and Capileira are among the villages that offer a glimpse into a way of life seemingly frozen in time. Take leisurely walks along ancient paths, where you'll encounter picturesque landscapes and encounter locals going about their daily routines.

The Alpujarra region is known for its traditional craft workshops, where artisans continue to practice ancient techniques. Visit these workshops to witness the creation of intricate textiles, pottery, and woodwork. The region's cuisine is also a delight, with dishes like Alpujarra-style migas (fried breadcrumbs) and cured ham showcasing the flavors and culinary traditions of the area.

Setenil de las Bodegas:

Setenil de las Bodegas is a captivating village that seems to defy the laws of architecture, as some of its houses are built directly into the rock face. The result is a unique blend of nature and human ingenuity that makes this village truly remarkable. As you wander through the narrow streets, marvel at the houses tucked beneath overhanging cliffs and appreciate the resourcefulness of the residents who have adapted to this extraordinary environment.

One of the highlights of Setenil de las Bodegas is the opportunity to dine in the rock. Several local restaurants are carved into the rock face, offering a dining experience unlike any other. Enjoy a meal in these cave-like establishments, where the coolness of the stone provides respite from the Andalusian heat. As you savor your meal, take a moment to appreciate the fascinating architecture and the ingenuity required to create such unique dining spaces.

Grazalema:

Tucked away in the heart of the Sierra de Grazalema Natural Park, the village of Grazalema offers a haven for nature lovers and outdoor enthusiasts. Surrounded by lush green landscapes and crisscrossed by hiking trails, this picturesque village invites you to explore its stunning natural scenery. Lace up your hiking boots and embark on one of the many trails that wind through the park, allowing you to discover hidden waterfalls, breathtaking viewpoints, and an abundance of flora and fauna.

Grazalema is also known for its traditional craft of wool weaving. Visit the local workshops to witness the artisans at work, using traditional looms to create beautiful textiles. Take home a piece of Grazalema's heritage by purchasing a handcrafted woolen item, such as a blanket or scarf, as a lasting memento of your visit.

Immerse yourself in the tranquility and beauty of the countryside as you explore Grazalema and its surrounding natural park. Breathe in the fresh mountain air, listen to the soothing sounds of nature, and allow yourself to be captivated by the serene charm of this hidden gem.

As you venture off the beaten path in Andalucia, keep in mind that these destinations may have a slower pace of life compared to the bustling cities. Embrace the opportunity to connect with the locals, savor the regional cuisine, and immerse yourself in the natural beauty that surrounds you. Whether you choose to explore the white-washed villages, drive through the scenic Alpujarra region, or discover the unique architecture of Setenil de las Bodegas, these hidden gems will reward you with unforgettable experiences and a deeper understanding of the diverse tapestry that is Andalucia.

Local Recommendations:

To truly immerse yourself in the local culture of Andalucia, one of the best ways is to connect with the locals themselves. Andalusians are known for their warm hospitality and friendly nature, and striking up conversations with them can lead to unforgettable experiences and insider recommendations that will enhance your journey through Southern Spain.

When you arrive in a new city or town, take the opportunity to engage with the locals. Start by greeting them with a friendly "Hola" (hello) or "Buenos días/tardes" (good morning/afternoon) and you'll often be met with a genuine smile and welcoming response. Don't hesitate to ask for recommendations or advice on where to eat, drink, and explore. Andalusians are proud of their region and love to share their favorite spots with visitors.

One of the best ways to seek recommendations from the locals is to visit local markets, cafes, and bars. These places are not only hubs of daily life but also offer a chance to mingle with the locals. Strike up conversations with the vendors at the markets and inquire about the freshest local produce, traditional dishes, or even recipes. You'll not only gain valuable insights into the local cuisine but might also find tips on lesser-known eateries or hidden gastronomic gems.

Cafes and bars are integral to Andalusian culture, where locals often gather to socialize and unwind. Sidle up to the bar, order a cup of café con leche or a refreshing glass of local wine, and strike up a conversation with the bartender or the person sitting next to you. They can provide insights into the city's nightlife, cultural events, and live music performances that may not be widely known to tourists.

In addition to personal recommendations, locals can also guide you to off-the-beaten-path attractions and hidden gems that may not be found in guidebooks. These can be secluded beaches, picturesque hiking trails, or quaint villages that showcase the true essence of Andalusian life. By venturing off the well-trodden tourist path, you'll have the opportunity to immerse yourself in the authentic local culture and witness the region's natural beauty and charm.

Keep in mind that many Andalusians have a siesta tradition, where they take a break in the afternoon to rest and recharge. During this time, you may find some establishments, especially smaller family-owned shops, closed for a few hours. Embrace this cultural practice and use it as an opportunity to explore local parks, stroll through the historic streets, or relax in a cozy plaza, observing the unhurried rhythm of daily life.

Andalusians are also proud of their regional festivals and celebrations, which are deeply rooted in their cultural heritage. If you have the chance to visit during a local festival or event, seize the opportunity to immerse yourself in the vibrant atmosphere. From the flamboyant Semana Santa processions to the lively Feria de Abril, these festivities offer a glimpse into Andalusia's traditions, music, dance, and gastronomy. The locals will be more than happy to share their customs and celebrations with you, providing an authentic and memorable experience.

To make the most of your interactions with locals, it's helpful to have a basic understanding of Spanish phrases. While many Andalusians can communicate in English to some extent, attempting a few words or phrases in their language shows respect and appreciation for their culture. Simple greetings, thank you ("gracias"), and phrases like "¿Dónde está...?" (Where is...?) or "¿Qué me recomienda?" (What do you recommend?) can go a long way in establishing a connection and eliciting a warm response.

Lastly, be open-minded and curious when engaging with the locals. Show genuine interest in their stories, traditions, and way of life. Andalusians are known for their passion for flamenco, bullfighting, and their regional identity. By demonstrating respect and appreciation for their cultural expressions, you'll be welcomed into their world and gain a deeper understanding of the Andalusian spirit.

Seeking recommendations from the locals in Andalucia is an excellent way to immerse yourself in the rich and diverse culture of the region. From hidden culinary delights to off-the-beaten-path attractions, the locals' insights can unveil a side of Andalusia that goes beyond the tourist highlights. Embrace the opportunity to engage with the friendly Andalusians, and you'll create meaningful connections, unforgettable memories, and a deeper appreciation for this captivating corner of Southern Spain.

In conclusion, Andalucia offers a wealth of experiences and treasures for travelers. By following these practical tips, you'll be well-prepared to navigate the region, engage with the local culture, and create unforgettable memories during your journey through the riches of Southern Spain. So pack your bags, embrace the Andalusian spirit, and get ready for an incredible adventure in this enchanting corner of the world.

Discovering the Soul of Andalucia: A Journey through Time and Culture

Delving into Andalucia's Moorish Legacy

Andalucia holds a rich and fascinating history that stretches back centuries. One of the most prominent chapters of its past is the era of Al-Andalus, the Islamic empire that flourished in the region from the 8th to the 15th century. Today, the echoes of this remarkable period can still be felt throughout Andalucia, particularly in its architecture, art, and cultural traditions. Exploring the remnants of Al-Andalus allows visitors to delve into a captivating world of intricate designs, serene courtyards, and mesmerizing historical sites.

One of the crown jewels of Andalucia's Moorish legacy is the Alhambra, an architectural masterpiece nestled in the heart of Granada. Recognized as a UNESCO World Heritage site, the Alhambra stands as a testament to the sophisticated and elegant design principles of Islamic architecture. As you approach its grand entrance, you will be immediately struck by the imposing fortress walls that guard this magnificent palace complex. Step inside, and a world of wonder unfolds before your eyes.

Wandering through the Alhambra's palaces, patios, and gardens, you will be entranced by the intricate geometric patterns, delicate stucco work, and tranquil water features.

The Nasrid Palaces, with their intricately carved ceilings, ornate archways, and lavish courtyards, showcase the pinnacle of Al-Andalusian craftsmanship. The Court of the Lions, with its iconic fountain supported by twelve marble lions, stands as a symbol of the palace's beauty and grandeur.

As you explore the Alhambra's Generalife gardens, a sense of tranquility and harmony washes over you. These lush gardens, carefully designed to provide respite and pleasure to the palace's inhabitants, offer a serene oasis filled with colorful flowers, fragrant citrus trees, and the soothing sound of fountains. Stroll through the paths, sit on a shaded bench, and take a moment to appreciate the symphony of nature and architecture that surrounds you.

Another architectural marvel that showcases Andalucia's Moorish legacy is the Mezquita in Cordoba. Originally built as a mosque during the 8th century, the Mezquita is a true testament to the rich cultural exchange that took place during Al-Andalus. The mosque's interior is a breathtaking sight to behold, with a vast expanse of horseshoe arches, columns, and intricate mosaics that create a mesmerizing forest-like effect. The sheer scale and beauty of the Mezquita leave visitors in awe, evoking a sense of reverence and wonder.

The Mezquita's transformation into a cathedral during the Reconquista is a testament to the evolving history of Andalucia. The juxtaposition of the Christian elements within the Islamic architecture creates a unique and harmonious blend of cultures. As you explore the Mezquita, you will find chapels, altars, and religious art interspersed among the arches and columns, representing the coexistence and integration of different faiths and traditions.

Beyond the Alhambra and the Mezquita, Andalucia offers numerous other sites that showcase its Moorish legacy. In Seville, the Giralda, originally the minaret of a mosque, now serves as the bell tower of the city's cathedral and offers panoramic views of the city. The Alcazar of Seville, with its stunning Mudéjar architecture and enchanting gardens, is another must-visit destination that allows visitors to immerse themselves in the region's history and culture.

The influence of Al-Andalus extends beyond architecture, seeping into the fabric of Andalucia's art and cultural traditions. The intricate geometrical designs found in the Alhambra and the Mezquita, for example, have inspired artists and artisans throughout the centuries. Today, you can see the echoes of this legacy in the vibrant ceramics, decorative tiles, and intricate woodwork that adorn buildings and handicrafts across Andalucia.

Additionally, the traditions of music, dance, and poetry that originated in Al-Andalus continue to thrive in the region. Flamenco, the passionate and expressive art form that has become synonymous with Andalucia, is believed to have Moorish influences. Tracing its roots back to the fusion of various cultural traditions, including Islamic, Gypsy, and Jewish, Flamenco embodies the emotional depth and artistic richness of the region.

To truly understand Andalucia's Moorish legacy, it is essential to immerse oneself in the local customs and festivals that celebrate this cultural heritage. From the colorful Feria de Abril in Seville, where locals don traditional attire and dance sevillanas, to the vibrant Corpus Christi processions in Granada, where the streets come alive with floral carpets, Andalucia's festivals offer a glimpse into the traditions and rituals that have been passed down through generations.

As you explore Andalucia's Moorish legacy, allow yourself to be transported back in time. Listen to the echoes of the past as you marvel at the architectural wonders, appreciate the beauty of intricate designs, and immerse yourself in the cultural traditions that have shaped this enchanting region. Through this journey, you will gain a deeper appreciation for the enduring impact of Al-Andalus and the rich tapestry of history and culture that defines Andalucia today.

Tracing the Footsteps of Flamenco

Flamenco, the passionate and expressive art form, finds its roots in Andalucia, specifically in the southern region of Spain. It is an art form that embodies the history, emotions, and cultural identity of the Andalucian people. To truly understand and appreciate Flamenco, one must immerse themselves in its rhythmic beats, heartfelt melodies, and captivating performances. Let us take you on a journey through the history and soul of Flamenco, where you will discover its birthplace, explore its different styles and techniques, engage with local artists, and experience the power and intensity that makes Flamenco an integral part of Andalucia's identity.

The vibrant neighborhood of Triana in Seville stands as the birthplace of Flamenco. Steeped in history and with a rich cultural heritage, Triana has nurtured generations of Flamenco artists. As you walk through the streets of Triana, you can feel the spirit of Flamenco lingering in the air. It is here that intimate tablaos, Flamenco venues, come alive with fiery performances, where artists pour their heart and soul into each movement, each note, and each word. These tablaos serve as sacred spaces where the art form thrives and where spectators can witness the raw power and emotional depth of Flamenco.

Engaging with local Flamenco artists is a transformative experience. They are the torchbearers of this ancient art form, preserving its traditions and pushing its boundaries. By interacting with these passionate artists, you can gain insights into their lives, their inspirations, and their artistic journeys. Many of them come from families with deep roots in Flamenco, with stories passed down from generation to generation. Through conversations and personal connections, you will discover the significance of Flamenco in their lives and how it has shaped their identity.

Learning about the different styles and techniques of Flamenco is an essential part of understanding its complexity. Each style, or "palos," carries its own unique rhythm, melody, and emotion. From the melancholic "soleá" to the vibrant "alegría" and the fiery "bulería," each palo evokes a distinct feeling and narrative. Local artists can guide you through the intricacies of Flamenco, explaining the significance of various movements, gestures, and musical elements. They can teach you the basic steps of Flamenco dance, helping you find your own rhythm and express your emotions through this captivating art form.

Experiencing the power and intensity of Flamenco firsthand is an unforgettable encounter. As the music starts, the palpable energy fills the room, and the dancers begin their mesmerizing performance. The combination of intricate footwork, hand clapping, soulful singing, and virtuosic guitar playing creates a sensory feast that transcends language and touches the depths of your soul. The emotions conveyed through Flamenco are raw, ranging from joy and passion to sorrow and longing. It is through this art form that the Andalucian people have channeled their emotions, telling stories of love, loss, resilience, and celebration.

Flamenco is not just a performance; it is a reflection of the history and struggles of Andalucia's people. It emerged as an expression of the hardships faced by marginalized communities, serving as a voice for the oppressed and the voiceless. Throughout its evolution, Flamenco has embodied the resilience and determination of the Andalucian people, celebrating their culture, traditions, and identity. It has transcended borders and gained international recognition, captivating audiences around the world with its profound artistic expression.

In Andalucia, Flamenco is more than entertainment; it is a way of life. It is woven into the fabric of society, present in festivals, gatherings, and everyday moments. It is a source of pride and a symbol of cultural heritage. Through Flamenco, the Andalucian people share their stories, preserve their traditions, and keep their vibrant culture alive.

So, as you delve into the history and soul of Flamenco in Andalucia, allow yourself to be captivated by its rhythms, moved by its melodies, and inspired by its artists. Experience the power and intensity that resonates within the heart of this ancient art form. By embracing Flamenco, you will gain a deeper understanding of Andalucia's people, their struggles, their resilience, and their profound connection to their cultural heritage. Flamenco is an invitation to explore the rich tapestry of emotions and stories that have shaped Andalucia, a testament to the enduring spirit of its people.

Embracing Andalucia's Gastronomic Traditions

Embark on a culinary adventure through the vibrant flavors of Andalucia, where the region's gastronomy is a true delight for the senses. As you journey through the diverse landscapes and cities, you will discover a rich tapestry of ingredients, cooking techniques, and traditional dishes that reflect the unique cultural heritage of the region.

Andalucia's culinary traditions are deeply rooted in its abundant natural resources and a history shaped by different civilizations. The region's olive oil production is renowned worldwide, and the rich, golden elixir is an essential component of Andalucian cuisine. The fertile lands yield an array of fresh fruits and vegetables, which form the base of many traditional dishes. The sun-ripened tomatoes, peppers, cucumbers, and garlic are transformed into refreshing gazpacho, a chilled vegetable soup that offers respite from the warm Andalucian summers.

One of the iconic dishes you must try is salmorejo, a refreshing tomato and bread soup originating from Cordoba. It is made with ripe tomatoes, garlic, olive oil, and day-old bread, resulting in a smooth and velvety consistency. Topped with diced cured ham and hard-boiled eggs, salmorejo is a true delight that encapsulates the essence of Andalucian flavors.

Seafood plays a prominent role in Andalucian gastronomy, thanks to the region's extensive coastline. The Mediterranean and Atlantic waters provide a bountiful array of fish and shellfish that are transformed into delectable dishes. One such delicacy is pescaíto frito, which refers to a variety of small fish that are lightly battered and fried to crispy perfection. Served with a squeeze of lemon, this dish showcases the simplicity and freshness of Andalucian seafood.

But it's not just the main dishes that capture the essence of Andalucia's culinary traditions; it's also the tapas culture that is deeply ingrained in the region's social fabric. In Andalucia, going for tapas is not just about the food; it's a way of life. Wander through the narrow streets of Seville, Granada, or Malaga, and you'll encounter a multitude of tapas bars offering a delightful assortment of small, flavorful bites. From the classic Spanish tortilla (potato omelet) to the spicy patatas bravas (fried potatoes with a spicy tomato sauce), the tapas culture allows you to sample a variety of dishes while enjoying the lively ambiance of the local bars.

As you indulge in the culinary delights of Andalucia, be sure to explore the region's world-renowned wines and sherries. Jerez de la Frontera, located in the province of Cadiz, is the birthplace of sherry production. Take a tour of the bodegas (wineries) and learn about the unique aging process that gives sherry its distinct flavors. From dry and crisp Fino to the rich and sweet Pedro Ximenez, there is a sherry to suit every palate. Pair your sherry with some local cheese, olives, and cured meats for a true Andalucian experience.

In addition to sherry, Andalucia boasts a diverse selection of wines. The region's vineyards, nestled in picturesque landscapes, produce wines that are gaining international recognition. From the robust red wines of the Sierra de Malaga to the crisp white wines of the Montilla-Moriles region, there are plenty of options to satisfy wine enthusiasts.

Andalucia's culinary traditions are not just about the food and drink; they are also intertwined with the region's vibrant festivals and cultural celebrations. The joyous Feria de Abril in Seville is a perfect example, where locals dress in traditional flamenco attire and gather in casetas (festive tents) to eat, drink, and dance. Semana Santa, the Holy Week processions that take place throughout Andalucia, are also a time when traditional dishes hold special significance. The Semana Santa menu often includes dishes like potaje de vigilia (a hearty chickpea stew) and torrijas (a type of French toast) that are traditionally prepared during this religious holiday.

Throughout the year, Andalucia's festivals and fairs provide an opportunity to sample regional specialties. The Cordoba Patio Festival is a feast for the senses, where the city's residents open their beautifully adorned patios to the public. The scent of jasmine and orange blossoms fills the air as visitors wander from one patio to another, marveling at the vibrant flowers and architectural beauty while enjoying traditional treats and refreshments.

In Andalucia, food is not just sustenance; it's a celebration of life and a way to connect with the region's history and culture. So, let your taste buds take a journey through Andalucia's culinary traditions as you savor the flavors of rich olive oils, aromatic spices, fresh seafood, succulent meats, and exquisite wines. Immerse yourself in the vibrant tapas culture, uncover the secrets of Andalucia's vineyards, and embrace the joyous spirit of the region's festivals and traditions. Your culinary adventure through Andalucia will undoubtedly be a feast for both the stomach and the soul.

Immersing in Local Festivals and Traditions

Andalucia, with its vibrant festivals and rich cultural heritage, offers visitors a unique opportunity to immerse themselves in the region's lively atmosphere and experience the magic of its traditions. From the exuberant Feria de Abril in Seville to the solemn processions of Semana Santa in cities like Seville, Malaga, and Granada, Andalucia's festivals showcase the essence of the region's vibrant spirit.

The Feria de Abril, held in Seville, is one of Andalucia's most renowned festivals. For a week in April, the city transforms into a spectacle of color, music, and dance. The streets come alive with locals dressed in traditional flamenco attire, showcasing their elegant dresses and dashing suits. Horse-drawn carriages parade through the fairgrounds, while the joyful rhythm of sevillanas, a traditional Andalusian dance, fills the air. Join in the festivities by dancing, indulging in local cuisine, and experiencing the contagious energy that permeates every corner of the fair.

Semana Santa, or Holy Week, is another significant festival celebrated throughout Andalucia. This deeply religious event takes place in the week leading up to Easter and is marked by solemn processions that commemorate the Passion of Christ. The processions feature elaborate floats, or pasos, adorned with religious imagery and carried through the streets by members of religious brotherhoods. The participants, dressed in traditional robes, march in unison to the beat of drums, creating a solemn and moving atmosphere. Witnessing these processions in cities like Seville, Malaga, or Granada offers a profound insight into Andalucia's religious devotion and cultural heritage.

One of the most enchanting festivals in Andalucia is the Cordoba Patio Festival. Taking place in May, this festival celebrates the beauty of Cordoba's traditional patios, or courtyards. During the festival, locals open their exquisitely adorned patios to the public, inviting visitors to stroll through a tapestry of colors, fragrances, and architectural marvels. The patios, typically decorated with vibrant flowers, ceramic tiles, and cooling fountains, offer a serene escape from the bustling city streets. The festival showcases the deep-rooted tradition of patio culture in Andalucia, where the outdoor spaces are considered extensions of the home and serve as gathering places for neighbors and friends.

In addition to these major festivals, Andalucia is also known for its joyous romerías, which are traditional pilgrimages to sacred sites. These gatherings combine religious devotion, folk traditions, and celebratory rituals. Romerías take place throughout the year in various locations, and each has its unique charm. Participants dress in traditional attire and make their way to the designated pilgrimage site, often accompanied by lively music and dancing. These pilgrimages offer a glimpse into the close connection between spirituality, community, and heritage in Andalucia.

Participating in Andalucia's festivals and traditions allows travelers to fully embrace the region's rich cultural heritage and vibrant spirit. It provides an immersive experience, where visitors can witness and engage with the customs, rituals, and passion that define Andalucian culture. From the lively ambiance of the Feria de Abril to the profound solemnity of Semana Santa, each festival offers a distinct window into the soul of Andalucia.

Moreover, these festivals serve as a testament to the region's history and the influences that have shaped Andalucia's identity. The festivals' vibrant colors, lively music, and expressive dances reflect the cultural fusion that has occurred over centuries, blending elements from the Moorish, Christian, and Gypsy traditions that have left their mark on the region. They also highlight the importance of community and the sense of belonging that permeates Andalucian society.

Beyond the visual and auditory spectacle, these festivals provide a unique opportunity to connect with locals and experience their warm hospitality. From sharing traditional dishes and drinks to engaging in conversations about the significance of each celebration, visitors can form meaningful connections and gain a deeper understanding of Andalucian culture. The festivals become a bridge that brings people together, transcending language and cultural barriers, and fostering a sense of unity and shared experience.

To fully immerse oneself in Andalucia's festivals, it is essential to plan your visit accordingly. Research the dates of the festivals you wish to attend and consider booking accommodations in advance, as these events attract a significant number of visitors. Familiarize yourself with the local customs and etiquette, such as appropriate dress codes and respectful behavior during religious processions. Additionally, be prepared to navigate crowded streets and embrace the spontaneous nature of these festivals, as they often unfold with delightful surprises and impromptu celebrations.

Andalucia's festivals and traditions offer an extraordinary opportunity to discover the soul of the region. From the enchanting Feria de Abril in Seville to the deeply moving processions of Semana Santa and the mesmerizing beauty of the Cordoba Patio Festival, these celebrations allow travelers to connect with the rich cultural heritage and vibrant spirit of Andalucia. By immersing themselves in the magic of these festivals and engaging with locals, visitors can create lasting memories and gain a profound appreciation for the traditions that make Andalucia truly unique.

Immerse Yourself in Andalucia: A Comprehensive Travel Companion

Planning Your Itinerary: From Coastal Charms to Inland Treasures

When it comes to exploring Andalucia, creating a well-rounded itinerary is key to fully immersing yourself in the region's diverse charms. This chapter will serve as your guide, helping you plan an itinerary that allows you to experience the best of both the coastal areas and the inland treasures that Andalucia has to offer.

Begin your journey by discovering the stunning coastal towns and cities that line the Costa del Sol, Costa de la Luz, and Costa Tropical. Along the Costa del Sol, you'll find the glamorous resort town of Marbella, known for its luxurious amenities and beautiful beaches. Enjoy the vibrant atmosphere, indulge in exquisite seafood, and soak up the Mediterranean sun. Further along the coast, the historic port city of Cadiz awaits, offering a fascinating blend of ancient history and modern charm. Explore its narrow streets, discover its cultural heritage, and enjoy breathtaking views of the Atlantic Ocean.

As you venture inland, you'll uncover the hidden treasures of Andalucia's picturesque countryside. The region is dotted with enchanting white villages, known as "pueblos blancos," nestled amidst rolling hills and olive groves. Take the time to visit these charming villages, such as Ronda, Grazalema, and Zahara de la Sierra. Wander through their narrow streets, admire their traditional whitewashed houses, and experience the warm hospitality of the locals. These villages provide an authentic glimpse into rural Andalucian life and offer breathtaking panoramic views of the surrounding landscapes.

No visit to Andalucia would be complete without exploring its iconic cities. Granada, with its world-famous Alhambra, is a must-visit destination. Immerse yourself in the beauty of this Moorish palace, stroll through its stunning gardens, and marvel at the intricate architectural details. Seville, the capital of Andalucia, boasts the majestic Alcazar, a UNESCO World Heritage Site, with its stunning gardens and rich history. Lose yourself in the labyrinthine streets of the Santa Cruz neighborhood, visit the magnificent Seville Cathedral, and witness the captivating flamenco performances. Cordoba, known for its Mezquita-Catedral, offers a blend of Islamic and Christian architecture. Explore its narrow alleyways, visit the charming patios adorned with flowers, and marvel at the grandeur of the Mezquita-Catedral, which showcases an awe-inspiring mix of styles.

While planning your itinerary, consider the best times to visit each destination. Summers can be hot in Andalucia, particularly along the coast, so plan accordingly if you prefer milder weather. Spring and autumn are popular seasons, offering pleasant temperatures and vibrant festivals. Winter is an excellent time to visit for those who enjoy a quieter experience and want to avoid the crowds.

To make the most of your time in Andalucia, it's important to optimize your itinerary. Prioritize the top attractions and must-see landmarks in each destination, ensuring that you allocate enough time for a meaningful experience. Explore the Alhambra's Nasrid Palaces, Generalife Gardens, and Alcazaba in Granada. In Seville, don't miss the chance to visit the Alcazar, climb the Giralda Tower, and explore the Plaza de España. In Cordoba, immerse yourself in the mesmerizing beauty of the Mezquita-Catedral and wander through the charming streets of the Jewish Quarter.

Additionally, consider including other notable sites and experiences that resonate with your interests. Explore the flamenco culture in its birthplace, attend a traditional show, or even take a flamenco dance class. Indulge in Andalucia's culinary delights by sampling tapas, paella, and traditional dishes like salmorejo and pescaíto frito. Consider adding a visit to the Sierra Nevada mountain range for hiking or skiing, or venture into the Doñana National Park for birdwatching and nature walks.

Navigating Andalucia's Transportation System

Getting around Andalucia is a breeze thanks to its well-developed transportation system. Whether you're exploring the vibrant cities, coastal towns, or picturesque countryside, this section will provide you with practical tips and information to navigate the region efficiently and make the most of your travel experience.

Andalucia offers a variety of transportation options to suit different preferences and budgets. One of the most convenient and efficient modes of transportation is the train. The high-speed AVE (Alta Velocidad Española) train network connects major Spanish cities, including Madrid, Barcelona, Seville, and Malaga, making it easy to travel to and from Andalucia. The AVE trains provide a comfortable and time-efficient way to explore the region and beyond.

Buses are another popular mode of transportation in Andalucia, offering extensive coverage and flexibility. The regional bus network connects even the smallest villages, allowing you to reach remote and off-the-beaten-path destinations. The buses are comfortable and equipped with modern amenities, ensuring a pleasant journey.

For travelers who prefer more independence and flexibility, renting a car is a great option. Andalucia's well-maintained road network allows for easy navigation between cities and towns. Renting a car gives you the freedom to explore at your own pace and visit hidden gems that may not be easily accessible by public transportation.

When planning your travel itinerary, it's essential to consider the major transportation hubs in Andalucia. The cities of Seville, Malaga, Granada, and Cordoba are well-connected and serve as transportation hubs with airports, train stations, and bus terminals. These hubs offer numerous transportation options to reach different destinations within Andalucia and other parts of Spain.

To make your travel experience even more convenient, it's worth exploring the various types of tickets and passes available. The Tarjeta Dorada, or Golden Card, is a discounted card specifically designed for senior travelers, offering reduced fares on trains and buses. The Andalucia Card is another valuable option, providing discounted entry to popular attractions and monuments across the region.

Public transportation in Andalucia offers several benefits, including cost-effectiveness and reduced environmental impact. Using buses and trains allows you to avoid parking hassles and traffic congestion, especially in city centers. It also provides an opportunity to interact with locals and experience the authentic rhythm of everyday life in Andalucia.

When planning day trips and excursions from major cities, such as Seville or Malaga, there are several enticing options to consider. You can take a train to the enchanting town of Ronda, known for its dramatic cliffside setting and the famous Puente Nuevo bridge. Another popular choice is visiting the stunning beaches of Tarifa, known as a windsurfing paradise and offering breathtaking views of the Strait of Gibraltar.

To make informed decisions about transportation, it's essential to consider factors such as travel time, cost, and convenience. Timetables and schedules for trains and buses are readily available online or at the respective stations. Planning your itinerary in advance and checking the frequency of transportation options will help you optimize your time and ensure a smooth travel experience.

Furthermore, it's worth noting that Andalucia's transportation system is well-integrated, allowing for seamless connections between different modes of transport. For example, you can easily combine a train journey with a short bus ride to reach more remote locations. By utilizing different transportation options, you can create a comprehensive itinerary that covers both the popular highlights and off-the-beaten-path destinations.

In conclusion, Andalucia's transportation system offers a range of options to suit every traveler's needs. Whether you prefer the convenience of trains, the extensive coverage of buses, or the flexibility of rental cars, you'll find a suitable mode of transportation to explore this captivating region. With careful planning and the information provided, you can navigate Andalucia efficiently and make the most of your travel adventure.

Accommodation Options and Recommendations

Choosing the right accommodation is crucial for a comfortable and enjoyable stay in Andalucia. With its rich history, diverse landscapes, and vibrant culture, this region of Southern Spain offers a wide range of accommodation options to suit every traveler's preferences and budget. In this section, we'll delve deeper into the different types of accommodations available, providing insights and recommendations to help you make the best choice for your Andalucian adventure.

One of the most charming accommodation options in Andalucia is the traditional Andalucian guesthouse, known as "casas rurales." These guesthouses are typically located in rural areas, offering a unique opportunity to immerse yourself in the local culture and experience the authentic way of life. Casas rurales are often converted from old farmhouses or historic buildings, retaining their traditional architecture and rustic charm. Staying in a casa rural allows you to escape the hustle and bustle of the cities and enjoy the tranquility of the countryside. You can expect warm hospitality, cozy rooms, and delicious homemade meals prepared with local ingredients. It's an excellent choice for those seeking a peaceful retreat and a deeper connection with the Andalucian way of life.

For those who prefer a blend of modern comfort and traditional aesthetics, boutique hotels in Andalucia offer a perfect choice. These hotels are often tucked away in historic buildings, such as renovated mansions, palaces, or convents. The owners pay meticulous attention to detail, creating a unique ambiance that reflects the region's cultural heritage. Each room is carefully designed, showcasing a harmonious fusion of contemporary amenities and traditional décor. Staying in a boutique hotel allows you to immerse yourself in the history and charm of Andalucia while enjoying the luxuries of modern living. These hotels often offer personalized services, exquisite dining options, and well-curated experiences to make your stay truly memorable.

Budget-conscious travelers and backpackers will find a variety of affordable accommodation options in Andalucia. Hostels and budget hotels are scattered throughout the region, providing comfortable and economical choices for accommodation. Hostels offer dormitory-style rooms, where you can meet fellow travelers and exchange stories and recommendations. Private rooms are also available in some hostels for those seeking a bit more privacy. Budget hotels, on the other hand, provide basic yet comfortable rooms at affordable rates. These accommodations are often located in convenient locations, close to transportation hubs and popular tourist attractions. While they may not offer lavish amenities, they provide a cozy place to rest after a day of exploration, making them ideal for travelers on a tight budget.

To ensure a convenient and enjoyable stay in Andalucia, it's essential to consider the location of your accommodation. Each city in Andalucia has its own unique neighborhoods and areas, each offering a distinct atmosphere and advantages. For example, in Seville, the Santa Cruz neighborhood is known for its narrow streets, charming squares, and proximity to the city's main attractions like the Alcazar and the Cathedral. The Triana neighborhood, located across the river, is famous for its lively atmosphere, flamenco bars, and local markets. In Granada, staying near the Albaicin neighborhood provides stunning views of the Alhambra and easy access to the historic center. It's important to research and choose the neighborhood that aligns with your interests and priorities, ensuring easy access to attractions, dining options, and transportation hubs.

Andalucia offers a diverse range of accommodations catering to different travel styles and interests. If you're seeking a beach getaway, seaside resorts along the Costa del Sol or the Costa de la Luz are ideal choices. These resorts offer a mix of relaxation, water sports, and vibrant nightlife, with a variety of accommodation options ranging from luxurious beachfront hotels to family-friendly resorts. If you prefer a peaceful retreat surrounded by nature, countryside accommodations provide a tranquil escape. You can find charming country houses, rural lodges, and eco-friendly retreats nestled amidst olive groves, vineyards, or rolling hills. These accommodations allow you to connect with nature, go for scenic hikes, or simply unwind in the peaceful surroundings. For those who prefer the vibrant energy of the city, city center accommodations in major cities like Seville, Malaga, or Cordoba provide easy access to cultural landmarks, shopping districts, and bustling nightlife. Whether you choose a modern hotel or a historic property, staying in the heart of the city allows you to fully immerse yourself in its vibrancy and charm.

When selecting accommodation, it's important to consider the amenities and services that will enhance your stay. Wi-Fi availability is a common necessity for most travelers, allowing you to stay connected and share your experiences. Many accommodations in Andalucia provide free Wi-Fi access, but it's always advisable to check for reliable connectivity before booking. Breakfast options can vary among accommodations, ranging from continental breakfasts to elaborate buffet spreads. If you have dietary restrictions or preferences, it's worth checking if the accommodation can accommodate your needs. Additionally, for individuals with special needs, accessibility is an important factor to consider. Some accommodations offer wheelchair-accessible rooms and facilities, ensuring a comfortable and inclusive stay for all guests. It's essential to communicate your specific requirements with the accommodation provider before making a reservation.

By considering the different types of accommodations available, understanding the popular neighborhoods and areas to stay in each city, and taking into account essential amenities and services, you'll be able to find the perfect place to stay and create unforgettable memories in Andalucia. Whether you choose to immerse yourself in the local culture at a traditional guesthouse, indulge in luxury at a boutique hotel, embrace budget-friendly options, or select accommodations based on your preferred location or travel style, Andalucia offers a wide range of choices to suit every traveler's needs.

Essential Travel Tips for Safety and Comfort

To ensure a safe and comfortable journey in Andalucia, it's essential to be well-prepared. In this section, we'll provide you with practical travel tips to enhance your experience and address common concerns.

When traveling to Andalucia, it's important to familiarize yourself with the local customs and etiquette to show respect for the region's rich cultural heritage. The Andalusian people are known for their warm hospitality, and understanding their customs will enhance your interactions and experiences. Here are a few key aspects to keep in mind:

Greetings: Andalusians are friendly and often greet each other with a kiss on both cheeks or a handshake. It is customary to offer a warm greeting when meeting someone for the first time or when entering a shop or restaurant. Remember to use formal greetings with older people or those in positions of authority.

Mealtime Etiquette: When dining in Andalucia, it's important to observe local dining customs. Spaniards usually eat their main meal during the afternoon, with dinner being a lighter affair. It is common to linger over meals and enjoy conversation, so don't rush through your dining experience. Additionally, it's considered polite to wait for the host or hostess to begin eating before you start.

Dress Code: Andalucia is a relatively casual region, but it's still important to dress appropriately, especially when visiting religious sites or attending formal events. Revealing clothing is generally frowned upon in churches or when visiting more traditional areas. It's always a good idea to carry a scarf or shawl to cover your shoulders or knees if needed.

Siesta Time: In Andalucia, the tradition of the siesta (mid-afternoon rest) is still observed in some areas, particularly in smaller towns and rural communities. During this time, many businesses, except for restaurants and essential services, may close for a couple of hours. It's advisable to plan your activities around these siesta hours or embrace the relaxed pace of life during this time.

Discover useful phrases in Spanish to help you navigate everyday situations and interact with locals:

While many people in Andalucia can communicate in English to some extent, making an effort to speak a few basic phrases in Spanish will go a long way in building connections and showing respect for the local culture. Here are some essential phrases to learn:

- Greetings:
- Hola: Hello
- Buenos días: Good morning
- Buenas tardes: Good afternoon/evening
- Buenas noches: Good night
- Adiós: Goodbye
- Polite Expressions:
- Por favor: Please
- Gracias: Thank you
- De nada: You're welcome
- Disculpe: Excuse me
- Basic Questions:
- ¿Dónde está...? - Where is...?
- ¿Cuánto cuesta? - How much does it cost?
- ¿Habla inglés? - Do you speak English?
- ¿Puede ayudarme? - Can you help me?
- Ordering Food and Drinks:
- Quisiera... - I would like...
- La cuenta, por favor - The bill, please
- Una cerveza, por favor - One beer, please
- ¿Tienen menú en inglés? - Do you have an English menu?

- Directions:
- ¿Cómo llego a...? - How do I get to...?
- A la izquierda: To the left
- A la derecha: To the right
- Recto: Straight ahead

Find information on currency exchange, tipping practices, and emergency contact numbers:

Currency Exchange:

The official currency of Spain is the Euro (€). It's advisable to exchange your currency for Euros before your trip or upon arrival at airports, banks, or authorized exchange offices. ATMs are widely available throughout Andalucia, providing a convenient way to withdraw cash in local currency.

Tipping Practices:

In Andalucia, tipping is appreciated but not mandatory. It's customary to leave a small tip for good service, usually rounding up the bill or leaving an extra 5-10% of the total amount. In restaurants, check if a service charge (propina) is already included in the bill. For taxi rides, rounding up to the nearest Euro is common.

Emergency Contact Numbers:

In case of emergencies, it's important to know the local contact numbers. The universal emergency number in Spain is 112, which can be dialed for police, fire, or medical emergencies. It's also advisable to have the contact information for your embassy or consulate readily available.

Get guidance on staying healthy during your trip, including tips for safe drinking water and recommendations for necessary vaccinations:

Staying healthy during your trip to Andalucia is essential to fully enjoy your travel experience. Here are some tips to help you stay in good health:

Safe Drinking Water:

Tap water in Andalucia is generally safe to drink, but if you prefer, you can purchase bottled water from supermarkets and convenience stores. It's always a good idea to carry a reusable water bottle and refill it as needed from trusted water sources.

Vaccinations:

Before traveling to Andalucia, it's recommended to check with your healthcare provider or a travel clinic regarding any necessary vaccinations. Routine vaccines, such as measles-mumps-rubella (MMR), diphtheria-tetanus-pertussis, and influenza, should be up to date. Hepatitis A and B vaccinations may also be recommended depending on your travel plans and personal medical history.

Sun Safety:

Andalucia is known for its sunny climate, so it's crucial to protect yourself from the sun's rays. Apply sunscreen with a high SPF, wear a wide-brimmed hat, sunglasses, and lightweight, breathable clothing to protect your skin from sunburn and potential heatstroke. Seek shade during the hottest hours of the day, and stay hydrated by drinking plenty of water.

Learn about the local climate and weather conditions, allowing you to pack appropriately and be prepared for any changes:

Andalucia experiences a Mediterranean climate, characterized by hot, dry summers and mild winters. However, due to the region's diverse geography, there are slight variations in weather conditions. Here's a general overview of the climate in Andalucia:

Summer (June to August): Summers in Andalucia are hot and dry, with temperatures often exceeding 30°C (86°F) and reaching even higher in inland areas. It's advisable to pack lightweight, breathable clothing, a hat, sunscreen, and sunglasses to protect yourself from the sun.

Spring (March to May) and Autumn (September to November): These seasons bring milder temperatures, making them ideal for outdoor activities. It's a good idea to pack layers to accommodate temperature fluctuations, as mornings and evenings can be cooler while afternoons are pleasantly warm.

Winter (December to February): Winters in Andalucia are generally mild, but temperatures can be cooler, especially in inland areas and higher elevations. It's advisable to pack a light jacket or sweater for cooler evenings and mornings.

Rainfall: The majority of rainfall in Andalucia occurs during the winter months, with occasional showers throughout the year. It's advisable to carry a compact umbrella or a waterproof jacket in case of unexpected rain.

Understanding the local climate and weather conditions will help you pack appropriate clothing and accessories for your trip, ensuring your comfort throughout your stay.

Understand the importance of travel insurance and what coverage to look for:

Travel insuranceis an essential aspect of any trip to Andalucia. It provides financial protection and peace of mind in case of unexpected events or emergencies. Here's what you should know about travel insurance:

Importance of Travel Insurance:

Travel insurance protects you against various risks that can disrupt or impact your trip. It typically covers medical expenses in case of illness or injury, trip cancellation or interruption, lost or delayed baggage, and emergency medical evacuation. Having travel insurance ensures that you are financially protected and can receive assistance when you need it the most.

Coverage to Look for:

When choosing travel insurance for your trip to Andalucia, consider the following coverage options:

Medical Coverage: Ensure that your policy provides adequate medical coverage, including emergency medical expenses, hospitalization, and repatriation in case of a medical emergency.

Trip Cancellation and Interruption: This coverage protects your financial investment in case you need to cancel or cut short your trip due to unforeseen circumstances, such as illness, injury, or a family emergency.

Baggage and Personal Belongings: Look for coverage that reimburses you for lost, stolen, or damaged baggage and personal belongings. This can include coverage for items such as cameras, electronics, and jewelry.

Emergency Evacuation: In the event of a medical emergency, having coverage for emergency medical evacuation ensures that you can be transported to the nearest suitable medical facility or even repatriated to your home country if necessary.

Travel Delay or Missed Connections: This coverage provides reimbursement for additional expenses incurred due to significant travel delays or missed connections, such as accommodation, meals, and transportation.

Safeguarding Your Belongings:

While exploring Andalucia, it's important to take precautions to safeguard your belongings. Here are some tips to help protect your valuables:

Use a Money Belt or Hidden Pouch: Keep your important documents (passport, credit cards, etc.) and extra cash in a concealed money belt or hidden pouch worn under your clothing.

Use Hotel Safes: Utilize the safe provided in your hotel room to store your valuable items, such as passports, jewelry, and extra cash.

Avoid Flashy Displays: Avoid drawing unnecessary attention to valuable items like cameras, smartphones, or expensive jewelry. Keep them discreetly stored when not in use.

Be Mindful in Crowded Areas: In crowded places, such as markets or public transportation, be vigilant about pickpockets. Keep your bags and wallets secure and close to your body.

Staying Vigilant Against Common Travel Scams:

While Andalucia is generally a safe destination, it's essential to stay vigilant against common travel scams. Here are a few tips to help you avoid falling victim to scams:

Be Cautious with Strangers: Exercise caution when approached by strangers offering unsolicited help or services. Always be aware of your surroundings and trust your instincts.

Use Official Transportation Services: When taking a taxi, ensure that it is a licensed taxi with a visible identification number and a working meter. Avoid unlicensed or unofficial transportation services.

Verify Prices and Bills: Double-check prices and bills before making a payment, especially in restaurants or tourist areas. Ensure that you understand any additional charges or fees.

Protect Your Personal Information: Be cautious when sharing personal information or credit card details, especially in public areas or over unsecured Wi-Fi networks.

Navigating Potential Language Barriers and Finding English-Speaking Services:

While English is widely spoken in tourist areas of Andalucia, it's helpful to be prepared for potential language barriers and know how to find English-speaking services. Here are some tips:

Learn Basic Spanish Phrases: Familiarize yourself with basic Spanish phrases, as mentioned earlier, to facilitate communication in everyday situations.

Use Translation Apps: Download translation apps on your smartphone to help with language barriers. These apps can be useful for translating menus, signs, or conversing with locals.

Seek Assistance from Tourist Information Centers: Tourist information centers are located in major cities and tourist hotspots. The staff there can provide assistance in English and help with any inquiries or concerns you may have.

Ask Your Hotel for Help: If you encounter difficulties communicating or need assistance, don't hesitate to ask the staff at your hotel. They often have experience with language barriers and can offer guidance or help you find English-speaking services.

By understanding the importance of travel insurance, safeguarding your belongings, staying vigilant against scams, and being prepared for potential language barriers, you'll be well-equipped to navigate Andalucia with confidence and ensure a safe and enjoyable trip.

From Flamenco to Tapas: Embrace the Essence of Andalucia

Exploring Andalucia's Vibrant Culinary Scene

Andalucia is a region that truly captures the essence of Spain's rich culinary heritage. With its diverse landscapes, from the stunning Mediterranean coast to the rugged mountain ranges, Andalucia offers a wide array of ingredients that have shaped its gastronomy over the centuries. Exploring the vibrant culinary scene of Andalucia is a delightful adventure that will take you on a journey through its history, culture, and flavors.

One of the highlights of Andalucian cuisine is its seafood. The coastal towns of Malaga and Cadiz are renowned for their fresh catch of the day. Stroll along the picturesque harbors, and you'll find bustling fish markets brimming with a vibrant selection of seafood, from plump prawns and succulent octopus to tender grilled sardines. Don't miss the famous Pescaíto frito, a medley of lightly battered and fried fish that is a true delight for seafood lovers.

Moving inland, the cities of Seville and Cordoba offer a different culinary experience, with a focus on hearty stews and succulent roasted meats. Seville is famous for its Gazpacho, a refreshing cold soup made with tomatoes, cucumbers, peppers, and olive oil. This Andalucian classic is a perfect choice for hot summer days. In Cordoba, the star dish is the Rabo de Toro, a rich and flavorful oxtail stew slow-cooked in red wine, vegetables, and aromatic herbs. The meat becomes tender and falls off the bone, creating a melt-in-your-mouth sensation.

Andalucia is also a land of olive groves, producing some of the finest olive oils in the world. The region's mild climate and fertile soil provide the perfect conditions for olive trees to thrive. The local olive oil, known as "liquid gold," is a staple ingredient in Andalucian cuisine. Its distinctive fruity and peppery flavors enhance every dish, from simple salads to hearty stews. Visit an olive mill and learn about the traditional production methods that have been passed down through generations, and sample the different varieties of olive oil for a truly authentic experience.

No culinary journey through Andalucia would be complete without indulging in the tradition of tapas. Tapas are small plates of food that are typically enjoyed with a glass of wine or a refreshing beer. This social and convivial dining style is deeply ingrained in Andalucian culture. In every town and city, you'll find lively tapas bars filled with locals and visitors, creating a vibrant atmosphere. The variety of tapas is endless, ranging from the classic Patatas bravas, fried potatoes with a spicy tomato sauce, to the delicate and flavorful Jamón ibérico, thinly sliced cured ham from acorn-fed Iberian pigs. Each bite tells a story, showcasing the region's culinary traditions and the skill of its chefs.

Andalucia's cuisine is not just about savory dishes; it also has a sweet side. The region is famous for its delectable desserts and pastries. Seville is the birthplace of the traditional Easter treat called Torrijas, a delicious bread pudding soaked in milk, flavored with cinnamon, and then fried to golden perfection. Another must-try dessert is the Polvorones, crumbly almond cookies dusted with powdered sugar, which are a staple during the Christmas season. Andalucia's sweets are a testament to the region's rich culinary heritage and the importance of celebrations and traditions.

To truly embrace the essence of Andalucia's culinary scene, one must also explore its rich beverage culture. The region is home to several renowned wine-producing areas, with Jerez de la Frontera at the forefront. Jerez is world-famous for its sherry wines, which are produced using a unique winemaking process known as the solera system. Take a tour of a bodega and witness the fascinating process of aging and blending these exquisite wines. From the bone-dry Fino and Manzanilla to the rich and sweet Pedro Ximénez, each sip reveals the complexity and craftsmanship behind these remarkable wines.

In addition to its wines, Andalucia offers a diverse selection of spirits. The region's brandies are particularly celebrated. Distilleries like Osborne and Lustau produce exquisite brandies that rival some of the best in the world. A glass of brandy from Andalucia is a perfect way to savor the moment and appreciate the region's dedication to craftsmanship.

Lastly, experiencing flamenco is an essential part of understanding Andalucia's culture and passion. Flamenco is not only a musical genre but also a way of life that encompasses music, dance, and emotion. It originated in the region and has become an internationally recognized art form. Attending a flamenco show allows you to witness the intense emotions conveyed through the powerful rhythms, soulful singing, and intricate dance movements. The energy and passion of the performers create an unforgettable experience that resonates with the vibrant spirit of Andalucia.

From its coastal delicacies to its hearty stews, Andalucia's culinary scene offers a tapestry of flavors and a glimpse into the region's rich cultural heritage. Exploring the vibrant markets, savoring tapas, indulging in local wines and spirits, and experiencing the passion of flamenco are all essential aspects of embracing the essence of Andalucia. So, embark on this gastronomic adventure and let your taste buds guide you through the diverse and tantalizing world of Andalucian cuisine.

Sampling Traditional Tapas and Local Delicacies

No visit to Andalucia is complete without indulging in the delightful world of tapas. Tapas, which originated in Spain, have become an integral part of Andalucian culture. These small plates of food, traditionally served with drinks, have evolved into a culinary experience that embodies the essence of sharing, socializing, and savoring the rich flavors of Andalucia.

As you wander through the narrow streets of charming towns and cities, you'll find bustling tapas bars that are a quintessential part of the local lifestyle. These lively establishments are filled with locals and visitors alike, creating a vibrant atmosphere that beckons you to join in and immerse yourself in the conviviality of Andalucian culture.

The beauty of tapas lies in their diversity and abundance. There is an endless variety of tapas to choose from, ensuring that there is something to please every palate. From the moment you step into a tapas bar, your senses will be overwhelmed by the tantalizing aromas and colorful displays of these bite-sized culinary treasures.

To truly appreciate Andalucia's culinary heritage, it is essential to sample the traditional tapas that have become icons of the region's gastronomy. One such classic tapa is patatas bravas, a beloved dish featuring crispy fried potatoes smothered in a spicy tomato sauce. The contrast between the crispy exterior and the soft interior, combined with the fiery sauce, creates a flavor explosion that is simply irresistible.

Another tapa that should not be missed is gambas al ajillo, a dish that showcases the region's abundant seafood. Succulent shrimp are sautéed in fragrant olive oil with garlic, chili peppers, and sometimes a splash of white wine. The aroma that fills the air as this dish sizzles on the stove is enough to awaken your appetite, and the combination of flavors will transport you to the Mediterranean coast with each delectable bite.

And of course, no discussion of Andalucian tapas would be complete without mentioning the world-renowned Jamón ibérico. This cured ham, made from acorn-fed Iberian pigs, is a true delicacy. The meat is marbled with flavorful fat, resulting in a melt-in-your-mouth texture and a complex, nutty flavor. Each bite of Jamón ibérico is a testament to the region's time-honored traditions of craftsmanship and culinary excellence.

But tapas in Andalucia are not limited to these iconic dishes. The culinary landscape is vast and diverse, offering a multitude of options to suit every taste. From fresh seafood like boquerones (marinated anchovies) and pulpo a la gallega (Galician-style octopus) to hearty meat dishes such as albóndigas (meatballs) and carrillada (braised pork cheeks), there is a tapa to satisfy every craving.

One of the joys of tapas is the opportunity to sample a variety of flavors and textures in one sitting. It is common to order several different tapas and share them among your companions, creating a communal dining experience that fosters conversation and camaraderie. Whether you're dining with friends or enjoying a solo adventure, tapas provide the perfect opportunity to explore Andalucia's culinary landscape at your own pace.

To accompany your tapas, be sure to try the local wines and spirits that perfectly complement the flavors of Andalucia. The region is known for its excellent wines, with Jerez de la Frontera being a particular highlight. This city is famous for its production of sherry, a fortified wine that comes in a range of styles, from dry and crisp fino to rich and sweet Pedro Ximénez. Sipping a glass of chilled sherry alongside your tapas is a match made in culinary heaven.

For those who prefer spirits, Andalucia is also home to some exceptional options. The region is renowned for its production of brandies, with Jerez once again taking the lead. These brandies are crafted using traditional methods, with time-honored aging techniques that result in smooth, complex flavors. Additionally, Andalucia boasts a thriving gin culture, with local distilleries producing a variety of aromatic gins infused with botanicals that reflect the region's unique terroir.

In addition to the culinary delights, experiencing flamenco is an integral part of immersing yourself in the essence of Andalucia. This passionate and expressive art form is deeply rooted in the region's history and culture. Just as tapas bring people together to share food and stories, flamenco brings people together through music, dance, and emotion.

Flamenco is an experience that transcends mere entertainment; it is a visceral connection to the soul of Andalucia. The music, characterized by the haunting sounds of the guitar, the rhythmic handclapping, and the soul-stirring vocals, has the power to evoke profound emotions. The dancers, with their precise footwork and dramatic gestures, bring the music to life, telling stories of love, pain, and longing.

Attending a flamenco show in Andalucia is an opportunity to witness the raw intensity and undeniable talent of the artists who dedicate their lives to this art form. From intimate performances in cozy venues to grand spectacles in historic theaters, the spirit of flamenco can be experienced in various settings throughout the region. The passion and energy of the performers are infectious, drawing the audience into a world of music, dance, and pure emotion.

To truly embrace the essence of Andalucia, one must partake in the delightful world of tapas, savoring the diverse flavors that showcase the region's culinary heritage. From the traditional favorites to the innovative creations, each tapa tells a story and invites you to explore the rich gastronomic tapestry of Andalucia. Paired with local wines and spirits and accompanied by the captivating rhythms of flamenco, this culinary journey through Andalucia will leave an indelible mark on your palate and your soul.

Sipping Andalucian Wines and Spirits

Andalucia's reputation for exceptional wines and spirits extends far beyond its culinary delights. The region boasts a rich tradition of winemaking and distilling, making it a paradise for oenophiles and spirits enthusiasts alike. From the world-famous sherry wines of Jerez de la Frontera to the flamboyant brandies and aromatic gins, Andalucia offers a diverse and captivating selection of libations that embody the region's cultural heritage.

One of the most renowned wine-producing areas in Andalucia is Jerez de la Frontera. This historic city, located in the province of Cadiz, is famous for its exquisite sherry wines. A visit to Jerez is an opportunity to immerse yourself in the fascinating world of sherry production and gain a deeper understanding of this ancient winemaking tradition.

Embarking on a tour of a bodega, or wine cellar, in Jerez is a journey into the heart of the sherry-making process. These bodegas, many of which have been family-owned for generations, offer a glimpse into the meticulous craftsmanship involved in producing sherry. Knowledgeable guides lead visitors through the vineyards, explaining the different grape varieties used and the unique terroir of the region.

Inside the bodega, visitors witness the various stages of winemaking, from fermentation to aging. Sherry is a fortified wine, meaning it is strengthened with distilled spirits, typically brandy, to increase its alcohol content and preserve its flavors. You'll learn about the solera system, a traditional method of blending and aging sherry, where barrels of different vintages are stacked in a series of tiers, allowing older wines to impart their character to younger ones.

As you explore the bodega, you'll have the opportunity to indulge in the distinct flavors of sherry through a tasting experience. Fino and oloroso are two popular styles of sherry, each with its own characteristics. Fino is pale, dry, and delicate, while oloroso is darker, richer, and more full-bodied. Sipping a glass of sherry allows you to appreciate the complexity and nuances of these exceptional wines.

Beyond sherry, Andalucia is also renowned for its production of brandies and gins. The region's brandies, known for their flamboyance and elegance, have a long-standing reputation for excellence. Local distilleries take pride in their artisanal approach, combining traditional techniques with modern innovation to create spirits of exceptional quality.

A visit to a brandy distillery in Andalucia unveils the meticulous process behind the production of this beloved spirit. From the selection of the finest grapes to the careful distillation and aging in oak barrels, every step is crafted with precision and expertise. As you delve into the world of brandy-making, you'll have the chance to witness the careful blending of different aged spirits to achieve the desired flavors and aromas.

Andalucia's aromatic gins are another highlight for spirits enthusiasts. The region's gin distilleries infuse their products with a wide range of botanicals, capturing the essence of Andalucia's diverse flora. Juniper berries, citrus fruits, and aromatic herbs are just a few of the ingredients that contribute to the unique profiles of these gins. A visit to a gin distillery allows you to witness the artistry of the distillation process and gain insight into the creative combinations of flavors that make Andalucian gins stand out.

Whether you prefer wine, brandy, or gin, Andalucia offers a vast selection to satisfy every palate. The region's winemakers and distillers are passionate about their craft, and their dedication shines through in the exceptional quality of their products. As you explore the various wineries and distilleries, you'll not only indulge in the flavors and aromas of Andalucian libations but also gain a deeper appreciation for the cultural heritage that underpins these age-old traditions.

To complement the tasting experiences, many wineries and distilleries also offer workshops and educational sessions, providing a deeper understanding of the production processes and the characteristics of the different libations. These immersive activities allow visitors to enhance their knowledge while engaging with experts who are eager to share their passion for their craft.

In addition to the tours and tastings, Andalucia hosts numerous wine and spirits festivals throughout the year, celebrating the region's rich viticultural and distilling traditions. These festivals provide an opportunity to sample a wide array of wines, brandies, and gins from different producers, all in one lively and festive atmosphere. It's a chance to mingle with fellow enthusiasts, learn from experts, and discover new favorites to take home as souvenirs.

Andalucia's wines and spirits encapsulate the region's cultural heritage and offer a sensory journey through its landscapes, traditions, and flavors. Whether you're a connoisseur or simply appreciate the pleasure of a well-crafted libation, exploring Andalucia's exceptional wineries, distilleries, and festivals will undoubtedly deepen your connection to the region and leave you with lasting memories of its vibrant and diverse culinary scene.

Experiencing Flamenco: Music, Dance, and Passion

Flamenco, with its raw emotion and powerful expression, is truly the beating heart of Andalucia. This passionate art form has captivated audiences worldwide, enchanting them with its mesmerizing performances. Immerse yourself in the spirit of flamenco, and you will discover a world where music, dance, and emotions intertwine to create an unforgettable experience.

To fully appreciate flamenco, attending a live show is a must. Andalucia is home to numerous vibrant tablaos, specialized venues that showcase flamenco performances. These tablaos provide an intimate setting where you can witness the artistry up close. From the moment the musicians strike the first chord on the guitar, you will be transported into a realm where time stands still, and the intensity of the music and dance takes hold of your senses.

The skillful footwork of the dancers is one of the hallmarks of flamenco. Their rhythmic stomping and intricate foot patterns create a percussive symphony that resonates with the passion of the music. As the dancers move with precision and grace, their feet become an extension of their emotions, conveying joy, sorrow, longing, and desire.

But flamenco is not just about the dance; it is equally about the heartfelt singing, known as cante. The soulful voices of flamenco singers reach deep into the core of human emotion, expressing a range of feelings that transcend language barriers. Their voices convey the pain of lost love, the yearning for freedom, and the celebration of life's joys. The singers, often accompanied by handclaps and rhythmic palmas, create a rich tapestry of sound that complements the dancers' movements.

Every flamenco performance is a unique expression of the artists' personal experiences and cultural heritage. It is a form of storytelling through music and dance, and each artist brings their individual style and interpretation to the stage. The intensity of the performance builds, drawing the audience into a shared emotional journey. It is a captivating experience that elicits a visceral response, stirring the soul and leaving a lasting impression.

While attending a flamenco show at a tablao is a popular way to experience this art form, Andalucia also offers the chance to stumble upon impromptu street performances. In picturesque plazas and winding alleys, you might encounter a spontaneous gathering of musicians, dancers, and onlookers. These spontaneous performances capture the essence of flamenco's improvisational nature and the sense of community it fosters. Join the crowd, feel the energy in the air, and let yourself be swept away by the impromptu magic of a street flamenco performance.

Flamenco is deeply rooted in Andalucia's history and culture. It evolved over centuries, influenced by the diverse cultural influences that shaped the region. The music and dance have origins in the Romani people, who arrived in Andalucia from North India centuries ago. Over time, flamenco absorbed elements from Moorish, Jewish, and Andalusian folk traditions, resulting in a rich and vibrant art form that is uniquely Andalucian.

Beyond the performances, you can delve deeper into the world of flamenco by exploring its history and significance. Visit museums dedicated to flamenco, such as the Museo del Baile Flamenco in Seville, where you can learn about the art form's origins, its evolution, and the prominent figures who have contributed to its legacy. Engage with local flamenco enthusiasts and experts who can share their knowledge and passion for this art form.

For those who seek a hands-on experience, Andalucia offers opportunities to learn flamenco. Many cities and towns have dance schools where you can take classes and workshops, immersing yourself in the techniques and rhythms under the guidance of experienced instructors. Through these lessons, you will gain a deeper understanding of the intricate footwork, the expressive hand movements, and the musicality that make flamenco so captivating.

Flamenco is more than just a performance; it is an embodiment of Andalucia's passionate spirit. It has become an iconic symbol of the region, carrying the weight of its history, culture, and identity. Experiencing flamenco in Andalucia is a profound journey, one that will leave an indelible mark on your soul. Whether you attend a flamenco show at a tablao, witness a spontaneous street performance, or even try your hand at learning the dance, you will come away with a deeper appreciation for the power of music, the art of dance, and the richness of Andalucian culture.

From flamenco to tapas, Andalucia's essence lies in its vibrant culinary scene, where flavors dance on your palate, and the rhythm of flamenco resonates in your soul. Indulge in the region's gastronomic delights, savor traditional tapas, sip local wines and spirits, and immerse yourself in the captivating world of flamenco. In doing so, you'll truly embrace the heart and soul of Andalucia.

Unforgettable Adventures Await: Exploring Andalucia's Natural Wonders

The Sierra Nevada: Hiking and Skiing in the South

The Sierra Nevada mountain range in Andalucia is a true haven for outdoor enthusiasts, offering a plethora of unforgettable adventures. Stretching across the southern region of Spain, the Sierra Nevada boasts majestic peaks, breathtaking landscapes, and a wealth of recreational opportunities for both hikers and skiers.

During the warmer months, the Sierra Nevada transforms into a hiker's paradise, attracting nature lovers from around the world. The network of trails crisscrossing the region caters to all levels of expertise, ensuring that everyone can find a suitable route to explore. Whether you prefer leisurely strolls through picturesque meadows or challenging ascents to the highest peaks, the Sierra Nevada offers a diverse range of hiking options.

As you embark on your hiking adventure, you'll be treated to awe-inspiring vistas, dramatic gorges, and crystal-clear lakes nestled within the mountains. The natural beauty of the Sierra Nevada is truly captivating, with its diverse flora and fauna adding to the allure. Keep an eye out for the rare Spanish ibex, soaring eagles, and vibrant wildflowers that adorn the landscape. The experience of immersing yourself in the pristine wilderness of the Sierra Nevada is nothing short of magical.

For those seeking an adrenaline rush and a taste of winter wonderland, the Sierra Nevada becomes a sought-after destination for skiing and snowboarding enthusiasts during the colder months. With its modern infrastructure and excellent snow conditions, the Sierra Nevada Ski Resort offers an exceptional skiing experience. Whether you're a beginner looking to take your first lessons or an experienced skier seeking adrenaline-pumping descents, the resort caters to all skill levels.

The Sierra Nevada Ski Resort features an extensive range of slopes, including gentle nursery slopes for beginners, intermediate pistes for those looking to improve their skills, and challenging black runs for the more experienced skiers. The resort's state-of-the-art facilities ensure a comfortable and enjoyable skiing experience, with a variety of ski lifts, ski schools, and equipment rental services available.

In addition to downhill skiing and snowboarding, the Sierra Nevada also offers opportunities for cross-country skiing, snowshoeing, and other winter activities. The vast snowy landscapes provide a serene and peaceful setting for exploration and adventure.

Beyond the exhilarating sports, the Sierra Nevada is also home to charming mountain villages that offer a glimpse into the region's rich cultural heritage. Pampaneira, Bubión, and Capileira are among the famous white-washed villages perched on the mountainside, offering a delightful blend of traditional architecture, local crafts, and warm hospitality. Take a break from the slopes or trails and immerse yourself in the local culture by visiting these quaint villages, sampling traditional cuisine, and interacting with the friendly locals.

No matter the season, the Sierra Nevada mountain range in Andalucia promises unforgettable adventures for all who visit. Its natural beauty, breathtaking landscapes, and diverse range of recreational activities make it a true paradise for outdoor enthusiasts. Whether you choose to hike through its dramatic gorges, immerse yourself in the vibrant flora and fauna, or carve your way down the slopes of the ski resort, the Sierra Nevada will leave a lasting impression and create memories that will stay with you forever.

Coastal Charms: Beaches and Water Activities

Andalucia's coastline is a treasure trove of stunning beaches and charming coastal towns, beckoning travelers with their scenic beauty and offering a plethora of water activities to indulge in. From the sun-kissed shores of the Costa del Sol to the tranquil allure of the Costa de la Luz, this region of Southern Spain is a haven for beach lovers and water enthusiasts.

The Costa del Sol, aptly named the "Sun Coast," lives up to its reputation with its abundant sunshine, warm climate, and an array of sandy beaches that stretch for miles along the Mediterranean Sea. From popular tourist hotspots to secluded retreats, the Costa del Sol offers a diverse range of beach experiences. If you're seeking a lively atmosphere, head to bustling beach promenades like Marbella or Torremolinos, where you can soak up the vibrant energy of beachfront bars, restaurants, and shops. Join in a game of beach volleyball, build sandcastles with your family, or simply relax under a colorful beach umbrella, savoring the gentle sea breeze.

For those in search of tranquility and seclusion, the Costa del Sol also offers hidden gems such as Nerja or Estepona, where you can escape the crowds and find a more intimate beach setting. These idyllic coves and bays are perfect for couples seeking a romantic retreat or nature lovers yearning to immerse themselves in the unspoiled coastal beauty. Enjoy the crystal-clear waters, go for a leisurely swim, or explore the underwater world through snorkeling or scuba diving.

Water sports enthusiasts will find plenty of opportunities to get their adrenaline pumping along the Costa del Sol. Paddleboarding, jet skiing, and windsurfing are just a few of the thrilling activities available. Rent a paddleboard and navigate the calm waters, feeling the invigorating sensation of gliding across the sea's surface. Hop on a jet ski and feel the exhilaration as you zoom through the waves, enjoying the refreshing spray on your face. And if you're an experienced windsurfer or eager to learn, the Costa del Sol's favorable wind conditions make it an ideal destination to catch the wind and ride the waves.

On the other hand, the Costa de la Luz, which translates to the "Coast of Light," offers a different ambiance altogether. This stretch of coastline, facing the Atlantic Ocean, exudes a more laid-back and unspoiled atmosphere. The beaches here are characterized by their pristine beauty, backed by rolling sand dunes and fragrant pine forests. As you stroll along the shoreline, the sound of crashing waves and the scent of saltwater mingling with the sweet aroma of pine create a serene and refreshing atmosphere.

The Costa de la Luz is a paradise for nature enthusiasts and those seeking a quieter beach experience. Explore the expansive stretches of sand, where you can find a secluded spot to unwind and connect with nature. Take long, leisurely walks along the shore, feeling the fine sand beneath your feet and enjoying the sweeping views of the Atlantic. The unspoiled surroundings are ideal for birdwatching, as the Costa de la Luz is a significant migratory route for a variety of bird species.

If you're an equestrian lover, don't miss the opportunity to go horseback riding along the beaches of the Costa de la Luz. Many equestrian centers offer guided horseback tours, allowing you to explore the coastline from a unique perspective. Feel the thrill of riding through the surf, as you and your horse become one with the rhythmic sounds of the ocean. It's an experience that combines the beauty of nature, the grace of horses, and the freedom of the open beach.

For those seeking a more active and adventurous beach experience, the strong Atlantic winds that sweep across the Costa de la Luz provide ideal conditions for kiteboarding. With vast expanses of open beach and consistent winds, this area has become a popular destination for kiteboarding enthusiasts. Whether you're a seasoned kiteboarder or a beginner looking to try this thrilling sport, the Costa de la Luz offers the perfect playground to ride the waves and feel the exhilaration of being propelled by the wind.

In addition to the natural beauty and recreational opportunities, both the Costa del Sol and the Costa de la Luz boast charming coastal towns that are worth exploring. From the whitewashed villages perched on cliffs to the vibrant fishing communities, these towns add a touch of authenticity to your coastal experience. Wander through the narrow cobblestone streets, savor fresh seafood at local restaurants, and immerse yourself in the laid-back lifestyle of the Andalusian coast.

Whether you choose the lively and sun-drenched Costa del Sol or the tranquil and unspoiled Costa de la Luz, Andalucia's coastline offers an enchanting blend of picturesque beaches, captivating water activities, and charming seaside towns. It's a destination where you can relax, rejuvenate, and create lasting memories of your unforgettable coastal adventures in Southern Spain.

Discovering Andalucia's National Parks and Biosphere Reserves

Andalucia, nestled in the southern region of Spain, is blessed with a remarkable array of national parks and biosphere reserves. These protected areas are a testament to the region's commitment to preserving its natural heritage and providing a sanctuary for a rich diversity of ecosystems. From rugged mountains to marshlands, dense forests to coastal wetlands, Andalucia's natural wonders are waiting to be explored.

One of the crown jewels of Andalucia's natural treasures is Doñana National Park. Designated as a UNESCO World Heritage Site, this expansive park covers an area of approximately 543 square kilometers (210 square miles) and serves as a crucial stopover for migratory birds on their annual journeys. The park's unique location, situated at the convergence of the Atlantic Ocean, the Guadalquivir River, and the Guadalquivir Marshes, creates a haven for countless bird species.

Upon entering Doñana National Park, visitors are greeted by a mesmerizing landscape of vast dune systems, lagoons, and marshes. The park's diverse habitats provide shelter and sustenance for an impressive array of birdlife. Ornithologists and nature enthusiasts alike will be captivated by the opportunity to spot graceful flamingos, majestic eagles, and countless other avian species. The sight of flocks of birds taking flight against the backdrop of the park's breathtaking scenery is truly awe-inspiring.

To fully appreciate the wonders of Doñana, it is highly recommended to join a guided tour led by knowledgeable experts. These guides provide invaluable insights into the park's delicate ecosystem, its significance for wildlife conservation, and the ongoing efforts to protect its fragile habitats. As you traverse the park's trails, your guide will share fascinating facts about the unique adaptations and behaviors of the birds and animals that call Doñana home. With their guidance, you can observe the intricate web of life that exists within the park and gain a deeper understanding of the importance of preserving these natural spaces.

Another natural gem in Andalucia is the Sierra de Grazalema Natural Park. Nestled in the province of Cadiz and part of the Sierra de Grazalema mountain range, this park is known for its awe-inspiring limestone landscapes and deep gorges. The park's rugged terrain is a paradise for hikers and nature lovers seeking to immerse themselves in its pristine beauty.

As you embark on a hike through Sierra de Grazalema, you'll be enchanted by the park's enchanting forests of Spanish fir and oak. These ancient woodlands provide a tranquil and shaded respite, inviting you to explore the trails at a leisurely pace. The park is also home to a rich variety of flora and fauna, including rare plant species that have adapted to the unique conditions of the limestone landscape.

One of the highlights of a visit to Sierra de Grazalema is the opportunity to witness the park's magnificent gorges. Among them, the Garganta Verde stands out as a natural wonder. This deep chasm, carved by the erosion of the Gaduares River, offers a breathtaking spectacle as you gaze down into its depths. The sheer cliffs rising on either side of the gorge create an imposing and awe-inspiring sight.

Scattered throughout Sierra de Grazalema are picturesque mountain villages that add to the park's charm. These whitewashed villages, such as Grazalema and Zahara de la Sierra, offer a glimpse into the traditional way of life in the region. With their narrow streets, charming architecture, and friendly locals, these villages are worth exploring and provide a delightful contrast to the rugged natural landscapes surrounding them.

Andalucia's national parks and biosphere reserves are a testament to the region's commitment to preserving its natural heritage. Doñana National Park and Sierra de Grazalema Natural Park are just two examples of the remarkable landscapes and biodiversity that await visitors. Whether you're a birdwatcher fascinated by the migration patterns of winged creatures or an avid hiker seeking to immerse yourself in rugged mountain scenery, Andalucia's natural wonders will leave you with indelible memories and a profound appreciation for the region's natural treasures.

Outdoor Excursions: Cycling, Horseback Riding, and More

Beyond hiking and skiing, Andalucia offers a plethora of outdoor activities that cater to the adventurous spirit. Whether you're seeking a leisurely exploration or an adrenaline-pumping experience, the region's diverse landscape and rich natural beauty provide endless opportunities for adventure seekers.

One of the most exhilarating ways to immerse yourself in Andalucia's countryside is through a horseback riding expedition. Saddle up and embark on a journey through the region's breathtaking countryside, where you'll traverse olive groves, vineyards, and rolling hills. The rhythmic trot of your horse will carry you along hidden trails and picturesque landscapes, allowing you to discover the rural charm that defines Andalucia. As you ride, take in the scent of wildflowers, feel the warm sun on your skin, and listen to the gentle breeze rustling through the trees. Horseback riding not only offers a unique way to experience the natural wonders of Andalucia but also allows you to connect with the region's rich equestrian heritage.

For cycling enthusiasts, Andalucia offers a wide variety of routes that cater to all preferences and skill levels. Whether you prefer scenic coastal paths or challenging mountain ascents, the region's diverse terrain ensures there is something for everyone. One notable cycling experience is the Via Verde, a network of converted railway tracks that crisscrosses through stunning landscapes and picturesque villages. The Via Verde provides a unique cycling experience, allowing you to pedal along historic railway lines while enjoying breathtaking views of Andalucia's natural wonders. Traverse lush valleys, pedal through tunnels, and pass by charming rural communities as you explore the region on two wheels. With well-marked paths and support facilities along the way, the Via Verde offers a convenient and enjoyable cycling adventure.

For those seeking an adrenaline rush, Andalucia offers a range of thrilling activities such as rock climbing, canyoning, and paragliding. The limestone cliffs of El Chorro are a mecca for rock climbers, with their vertical walls and challenging routes attracting climbers from around the world. Test your skills and push your limits as you scale the cliffs, surrounded by stunning panoramic views of rugged landscapes. Canyoning is another exciting option, allowing you to navigate through narrow gorges, rappel down waterfalls, and swim in natural pools. Experience the rush of adrenaline as you descend into deep canyons, exploring Andalucia's hidden natural wonders. Paragliding offers a unique perspective of the region, as you soar above the landscapes of Algodonales, taking in panoramic views of rolling hills, picturesque villages, and vast open spaces. Feel the wind beneath your wings as you glide through the sky, experiencing the freedom and exhilaration that only paragliding can provide.

No matter which adventure activity you choose, Andalucia's natural wonders are guaranteed to captivate your senses and leave a lasting impression. The region's diverse landscapes, from the rugged mountains of the Sierra Nevada to the tranquil beaches of the Costa del Sol, provide a stunning backdrop for outdoor enthusiasts. As you engage in these activities, take a moment to appreciate the beauty and biodiversity that surrounds you. Observe the unique flora and fauna, marvel at the geological formations, and connect with the natural world on a deeper level.

Andalucia's outdoor adventures not only offer thrilling experiences but also provide an opportunity to connect with the region's rich cultural heritage. Along your journey, you'll encounter charming rural communities, where traditions and customs have been preserved for centuries. Interact with friendly locals, savor traditional cuisine, and gain insights into the way of life in rural Andalucia. These authentic encounters will enhance your adventure, adding a cultural dimension to your exploration of the region.

Andalucia is a paradise for adventure seekers, offering a wide range of outdoor activities that allow you to explore its natural wonders from various perspectives. Whether you choose to embark on a horseback riding expedition through the countryside, pedal along scenic cycling routes, or engage in adrenaline-pumping activities such as rock climbing or paragliding, each experience will leave you with unforgettable memories. Immerse yourself in Andalucia's diverse landscapes, connect with its rich cultural heritage, and let the region's natural wonders captivate your senses. Andalucia truly is an adventurer's playground, waiting to be discovered and explored.

.

Beyond the Alhambra: Unlocking Andalucia's Architectural Gems

The Alcazar of Seville: A Royal Retreat

Nestled in the heart of Seville, the Alcazar is a mesmerizing architectural gem that stands as a testament to Andalucia's rich history and cultural heritage. This royal palace complex, with its exquisite blend of Moorish and Renaissance styles, offers visitors a captivating journey through time, immersing them in the opulent world of Andalucia's past.

As you step inside the Alcazar, you are instantly transported to a world of enchantment. The grandeur of the palace is complemented by its lush gardens, adorned with vibrant flowers and tranquil fountains. The scent of orange blossoms lingers in the air, creating a sensory experience that heightens the magic of the surroundings.

Explore the intricately designed halls of the Alcazar, where every inch is adorned with exquisite craftsmanship. Delicate stucco work, intricate tile patterns, and ornate arches showcase the artistry and attention to detail that went into creating this architectural masterpiece. Each hall tells a story of the different cultures and epochs that shaped the Alcazar, offering a glimpse into the historical tapestry of Andalucia.

One of the highlights of the Alcazar is the Palacio de Don Pedro, a true gem within the complex. This palace, with its lavish decorations and intricate detailing, served as the residence of various Moorish and Christian monarchs throughout history. Step into the Salón de los Embajadores (Hall of Ambassadors), and you'll be awestruck by the breathtaking golden dome and the mesmerizing star-shaped vault, adorned with delicate geometric patterns. The Mudéjar craftsmanship on display here is a testament to the skilled artisans who contributed to the Alcazar's construction.

However, the enchantment of the Alcazar extends beyond its palatial halls. The gardens of the Alcazar are a paradise unto themselves, with surprises awaiting at every turn. The Patio de las Doncellas (Courtyard of the Maidens) invites you to pause and soak in its tranquil beauty. The central pond, surrounded by lush greenery and delicate arches, reflects the elegance of the surrounding structures, creating a serene atmosphere that invites contemplation.

Stroll through the Jardines de Murillo, a vibrant oasis filled with colorful blooms and manicured hedges. Discover hidden corners, adorned with secluded fountains and charming alcoves, offering moments of tranquility amidst the bustling palace complex. These gardens not only serve as a visual delight but also provide a respite from the heat of Seville, offering shade and cool breezes that make the Alcazar a haven during the scorching Andalusian summers.

Every visit to the Alcazar is a unique experience, as the changing seasons bring their own beauty to the gardens. Spring paints the Alcazar in a riot of colors, with blossoming flowers and fragrant blooms. Summer brings lush greenery and provides an escape from the sun-drenched streets of Seville. Autumn casts a golden hue over the gardens, while winter adds a touch of tranquility, with its crisp air and fewer crowds.

As you wander through the Alcazar, it's impossible not to be enchanted by its timeless beauty. Each corner unveils architectural marvels and natural wonders, creating a harmonious blend of human ingenuity and the gifts of nature. The Alcazar stands as a living testament to the cultural fusion and exchange that took place in Andalucia, where Moorish, Christian, and Renaissance influences seamlessly intertwine.

The Alcazar is not merely a static monument frozen in time; it is a living entity that continues to inspire and captivate. Its allure has attracted artists, writers, and filmmakers who have sought to capture its essence and convey its enchantment to the world. The palace complex has served as a backdrop for numerous films and TV shows, further cementing its status as an iconic symbol of Andalucia.

A visit to the Alcazar is a journey into the heart and soul of Andalucia, where history, art, and nature intertwine to create an unforgettable experience. It is a place that invites you to slow down, to marvel at the intricacies of the past, and to immerse yourself in the beauty that surrounds you. The Alcazar of Seville is a true architectural gem, a treasure that unlocks the secrets of Andalucia's rich cultural heritage and leaves a lasting impression on all who have the privilege to explore its hallowed halls and enchanting gardens.

The Great Mosque of Cordoba: A Testament to Islamic Architecture

Prepare to be awestruck as you step through the doors of the Great Mosque of Cordoba, also known as the Mezquita. This architectural masterpiece stands as a magnificent example of

Islamic art and craftsmanship, representing the golden era of Al-Andalus.

Originally constructed as a mosque in the 8th century during the reign of Abd al-Rahman I, the Great Mosque underwent several expansions over the centuries, reflecting the influence of different ruling dynasties and architectural styles. What you see today is the result of the harmonious blend of Islamic, Christian, and Renaissance elements, a testament to the rich history and cultural diversity of Andalucia.

As you venture into the vast prayer hall of the Great Mosque, prepare to be enveloped by a sense of awe and tranquility. The hall boasts an impressive forest of columns, numbering over eight hundred, that support the intricately decorated arches above. Each column is a unique work of art, as they were sourced from various Roman, Visigothic, and Byzantine buildings, imbuing the mosque with a profound historical significance.

Among the mesmerizing architectural features, the horseshoe arches stand out as an iconic hallmark of Moorish design. These graceful arches, adorned with delicate carvings and intricate patterns, create a captivating visual rhythm throughout the prayer hall. As you explore further, you'll encounter double arches, an architectural innovation that adds depth and elegance to the space.

At the heart of the Great Mosque lies the Cathedral of Cordoba, an awe-inspiring Christian structure seamlessly integrated within the mosque's original architecture. Known as the Capilla Mayor, the cathedral occupies the former central nave of the mosque. Its construction was ordered by King Ferdinand III of Castile after the Christian Reconquista in the 13th century. The juxtaposition of the two religions within the same space creates a unique and harmonious ambiance, reflecting the historical coexistence of cultures in Andalucia.

Inside the cathedral, you'll discover a magnificent altarpiece and chapels adorned with intricate sculptures and ornate decorations. The high altar, dedicated to the Assumption of the Virgin Mary, features a splendid retablo crafted by renowned Renaissance artist Alonso Matías. The transition from the serene and tranquil mosque to the grandeur of the cathedral creates a powerful sensory experience, where one can witness the layers of history and spirituality that have shaped this sacred space.

For a panoramic view of Cordoba's enchanting cityscape, make your way to the minaret, known as the Tower of the Bell. Climb the winding staircase to reach the top and be rewarded with a breathtaking panorama that stretches as far as the eye can see. From this vantage point, you'll gain a new perspective on the city's rich tapestry of history and architectural wonders. The red-tiled rooftops, narrow streets, and the Guadalquivir River winding through the cityscape create a mesmerizing backdrop against which the Great Mosque and Cathedral stand tall.

As you explore the Great Mosque of Cordoba, take a moment to appreciate the cultural significance and historical legacy it represents. The mosque's transformation into a cathedral encapsulates the complex and interwoven histories of different civilizations that have left their mark on Andalucia. It serves as a symbol of tolerance, unity, and artistic excellence, offering visitors a unique opportunity to immerse themselves in the shared heritage of humanity.

Visiting the Great Mosque of Cordoba is not just an architectural exploration; it's a spiritual journey, a cultural pilgrimage that allows you to witness the magnificence of Islamic and Christian civilizations converging in one extraordinary space. It is an experience that will leave an indelible mark on your memory and deepen your appreciation for the rich tapestry of Andalucia's past.

The Cathedral of Malaga: Gothic Grandeur

Dominating Malaga's skyline, the Cathedral of Malaga, also known as La Manquita, meaning "the one-armed lady," is a masterpiece of Gothic architecture that captivates visitors with its grandeur and tells a fascinating story through its unfinished southern tower. Stepping inside the cathedral, one cannot help but feel overwhelmed by the sheer scale and beauty of the interior.

The moment you enter, your eyes are drawn upward to the soaring vaulted ceilings that seem to touch the heavens. The intricate stone tracery, delicate rib vaults, and elegant flying buttresses are testaments to the architectural skill and craftsmanship of the builders. Sunlight filters through the magnificent stained glass windows, casting a kaleidoscope of colors onto the stone floor, creating an ethereal atmosphere that invites contemplation and reflection.

As you explore further, your gaze is inevitably drawn to the ornate altarpieces that adorn the cathedral. These masterpieces of religious art, created by renowned artists of the time, depict scenes from the life of Christ, the Virgin Mary, and various saints. The level of detail and craftsmanship is awe-inspiring, with delicate carvings and intricate gilding that reflect the devotion and dedication of the artists.

One of the highlights of the Cathedral of Malaga is the majestic choir stalls, located in the central nave. Intricately carved with scenes from the Bible and adorned with statues of saints and apostles, these choir stalls showcase the incredible talent and artistry of the craftsmen who created them. The attention to detail is extraordinary, with every figure and ornament meticulously carved to perfection.

The cathedral is also home to numerous chapels dedicated to different saints and religious figures. Each chapel has its own unique character and style, with beautiful altarpieces, sculptures, and paintings that showcase the rich religious heritage of Malaga. These chapels offer moments of quiet contemplation and provide a glimpse into the deep spirituality that permeates the cathedral.

To truly appreciate the Cathedral of Malaga, visitors should not miss the opportunity to climb to the rooftop. As you ascend the narrow staircase, the views become increasingly breathtaking. From the top, you are treated to panoramic vistas of Malaga's cityscape, with its sea of whitewashed buildings, bustling streets, and the glistening waters of the Mediterranean stretching out to the horizon. The rooftop provides a unique perspective on the architectural feat that is La Manquita, and you gain a deeper appreciation for the monumental task undertaken by the builders who worked tirelessly to create this awe-inspiring structure.

The story behind the unfinished southern tower adds an intriguing layer of history to the Cathedral of Malaga. Construction of the tower began in the 18th century but was never completed due to financial constraints and a shift in architectural styles. Despite its incomplete state, the cathedral stands as a testament to the determination and resilience of the people of Malaga, who embraced this unique characteristic as part of their identity. The nickname "La Manquita" affectionately refers to the unfinished tower and has become a symbol of the city's pride and history.

As you immerse yourself in the Cathedral of Malaga, you can't help but feel a sense of awe and reverence. It is a place where centuries of faith, art, and history converge, creating a sacred space that resonates with visitors from all walks of life. Whether you are a devout believer, an art enthusiast, or simply a curious traveler, the Cathedral of Malaga invites you to step into its hallowed halls and be transported to a world of architectural magnificence and spiritual contemplation.

Ronda's Puente Nuevo: The Bridge to Andalucia's Past

Perched high above the dramatic El Tajo Gorge, the Puente Nuevo in Ronda is an architectural marvel that connects the city's historical districts and offers stunning vistas of the surrounding countryside. With its impressive design and breathtaking views, the Puente Nuevo has become an iconic symbol of Ronda, capturing the hearts and imaginations of all who visit.

Built in the 18th century, the Puente Nuevo stands as a striking example of Spanish architecture. Its construction was a testament to the engineering prowess of its time, as it was a challenging feat to build a bridge that spans the deep and rugged El Tajo Gorge. The bridge was designed by José Martín de Aldehuela and took over forty years to complete. Its construction required great skill and determination, as workers labored to overcome the formidable obstacles presented by the natural landscape.

As you walk across the Puente Nuevo, you are greeted with a panoramic view that leaves you breathless. The rugged cliffs of the El Tajo Gorge plunge dramatically below, and the Guadalevín River flows peacefully beneath the bridge. The vista extends to the picturesque white-washed houses that dot the city, creating a picturesque backdrop against the natural beauty of the surrounding landscape. The combination of architectural splendor and breathtaking scenery creates an experience that is truly unforgettable.

For a different perspective, venture down the stairs carved into the cliffs to reach the bottom of the gorge. From here, you can gaze up at the Puente Nuevo, marveling at its towering presence and appreciating the immense effort that went into its construction. The raw power of the natural surroundings, with the cliffs towering above and the river flowing steadily, adds to the awe-inspiring ambiance. It is a place where the forces of nature and human ingenuity intersect, leaving you with a deep sense of wonder.

Beyond its aesthetic appeal, the Puente Nuevo holds a significant historical value for the people of Ronda. It stands as a testament to their resilience and ingenuity, reflecting the city's rich past and its ability to overcome challenges throughout history. The bridge serves as a reminder of the determination and skill of those who came before, leaving a lasting legacy for generations to admire and appreciate.

Throughout the years, the Puente Nuevo has witnessed the ebb and flow of Ronda's history. It has withstood the test of time, surviving wars, political changes, and natural disasters. Its enduring presence is a symbol of the strength and endurance of the city and its people.

Today, the Puente Nuevo is not only a marvel of engineering and a historical landmark but also a beloved gathering place for locals and tourists alike. Visitors flock to the bridge to soak in its beauty, capture stunning photographs, and experience the thrill of standing suspended above the gorge. It has become an iconic symbol of Ronda, drawing people from all over the world to admire its grandeur and appreciate its significance.

As you stand on the Puente Nuevo, taking in the panoramic views and feeling the weight of history beneath your feet, you can't help but be moved by the splendor of this architectural masterpiece. It is a testament to human creativity and determination, showcasing the remarkable achievements that can arise from the collaboration between nature and human endeavor.

The Puente Nuevo is more than just a bridge. It is a gateway to Ronda's past, a connection between its historical districts, and a symbol of the city's strength and resilience. It invites visitors to contemplate the harmony between human creation and the natural world, leaving an indelible mark on their memories and reminding them of the power of human ingenuity.

A visit to Ronda is incomplete without experiencing the Puente Nuevo. It is a place where history, architecture, and natural beauty converge, creating an atmosphere of wonder and appreciation. Whether you are an architecture enthusiast, a history buff, or simply a traveler seeking awe-inspiring sights, the Puente Nuevo will captivate your senses and leave you with a deep appreciation for the enduring spirit of Ronda and its remarkable architectural gem.

Unlocking Andalucia's architectural gems is a journey that will transport you through time and immerse you in the region's captivating history and cultural heritage. Each architectural wonder holds its own unique story, waiting to be discovered and appreciated by those who venture to explore Andalucia.

Tantalizing Tastes and Vibrant Festivals: A Taste of Andalucia's Culinary Delights

Andalucian Gastronomy: A Fusion of Flavors

Andalucia, situated in the southern part of Spain, is renowned for its vibrant culinary scene that showcases a delightful fusion of flavors influenced by its rich history and diverse cultural heritage. Spanning from hearty stews to fresh seafood dishes, Andalucian gastronomy captivates the taste buds with its diverse and bountiful produce.

One cannot embark on a culinary journey through Andalucia without sampling the iconic Gazpacho, a refreshing cold tomato soup that epitomizes the region's commitment to utilizing fresh and seasonal ingredients. Made with ripe tomatoes, cucumbers, bell peppers, garlic, and olive oil, Gazpacho is a summertime favorite, offering a burst of flavors and a cooling sensation on hot Andalucian days. Similarly, the flavorsome Salmorejo, a thick tomato-based soup, often served with crusty bread and an array of toppings such as hard-boiled eggs, Serrano ham, and diced vegetables, is a must-try dish that perfectly embodies Andalucia's culinary prowess.

No visit to Andalucia is complete without immersing oneself in the world of tapas. These small plates of culinary wonders have become a hallmark of Spanish cuisine, and Andalucia takes pride in its exceptional tapas offerings. Picture yourself in a bustling tapas bar, surrounded by the chatter of locals, as you indulge in a plate of Jamón Ibérico, a succulent cured ham that melts in your mouth, or sample the marinated olives bursting with flavors. From mouthwatering patatas bravas (fried potatoes with a spicy tomato sauce) to delectable grilled vegetables, Andalucian tapas are a culinary adventure that showcases the region's rich culinary heritage in bite-sized portions.

For those who adore seafood, Andalucia's coastal areas are a treasure trove of culinary delights. Along the sandy shores, you will find the famous Espetos, grilled sardines skewered on a stick and cooked over an open fire. This traditional method of grilling imparts a smoky flavor and tender texture to the sardines, making them a true delicacy. Another seafood favorite is Pescaíto frito, a crispy fried assortment of seafood that includes shrimp, calamari, and small fish. Served with a squeeze of lemon, this dish is a delight for seafood enthusiasts, providing a tantalizing taste of the Mediterranean.

One cannot fully appreciate Andalucia's culinary landscape without acknowledging the profound influence of Moorish traditions. The Moorish rule, which lasted for several centuries, left an indelible mark on the region's cuisine. Delve into the aromatic and spiced world of Moroccan-inspired dishes like Tagine, a slow-cooked stew featuring tender meat, aromatic spices, and dried fruits. The flavors intertwine to create a harmony that tantalizes the taste buds and transports you to the exotic lands that once shaped Andalucia's culinary heritage. Another Moorish-inspired delight is Almond Chicken, where succulent chicken is cooked with ground almonds, saffron, and a medley of spices, resulting in a dish that is both rich in flavor and wonderfully aromatic.

Indulging the sweet tooth is an essential part of any culinary adventure, and Andalucia offers a plethora of regional desserts to satisfy even the most discerning palate. One such delight is Leche Frita, a creamy dessert made with thickened milk, flavored with cinnamon and lemon, and then lightly fried to create a crispy exterior. Served with a sprinkle of powdered sugar, Leche Frita is a comfort food that provides a heavenly combination of textures and flavors. Pestiños, honey-coated pastries, are another beloved treat. These delicate pastries are fried until golden and then drenched in a generous amount of honey, offering a delightful balance of sweetness and a subtle hint of spice.

Exploring Andalucia's culinary landscape is an invitation to savor a rich tapestry of flavors and traditions. From the refreshing and vibrant Gazpacho to the succulent Almond Chicken, each dish reflects the region's deep-rooted history and cultural influences. Embark on this gastronomic adventure and let the fusion of flavors guide you through the culinary delights of Andalucia.

The Feria de Abril: Seville's Flamboyant Spring Fair

The Feria de Abril, Seville's most anticipated event, is a week-long extravaganza that captures the true essence of Andalucian culture, flamenco music, and vibrant festivities. Held annually in April, this grand fair transforms the city into a magical spectacle of lights, colors, and unbridled joy, attracting both locals and visitors from around the world.

As the Feria de Abril commences, the fairgrounds burst to life with rows upon rows of brightly colored tents, known as casetas, creating a vibrant and festive atmosphere. These casetas serve as gathering places where families, friends, and communities come together to revel in the celebrations. Intricate decorations adorn the casetas, with vibrant fabrics, lanterns, and flowers adorning the interior and exterior, adding to the allure and charm of the fair.

The heart and soul of the Feria de Abril lie in its pulsating music and dance. The air resonates with the rhythmic beats of flamenco, the traditional music of Andalucia. Skilled musicians strum guitars, play castanets, and accompany soul-stirring singing, filling the atmosphere with passion and emotion. Flamenco dancers showcase their exquisite footwork and graceful movements, captivating the audience with their captivating performances.

As visitors wander through the casetas, they are greeted by an array of tantalizing aromas and flavors. The Feria de Abril is a gastronomic paradise, where the casetas offer a wide selection of traditional Andalucian dishes and drinks. One cannot resist trying the famous rebujito, a refreshing mix of sherry wine and soda, which is the quintessential drink of the fair. The aroma of sizzling grills tempts the taste buds as succulent grilled meats, such as the flavorful Rabo de Toro (oxtail stew) or mouthwatering Pinchos Morunos (spiced pork skewers), are prepared to perfection. Other traditional delicacies like Paella, Tortilla Española (Spanish omelet), and Salmorejo (thick tomato-based soup) are also popular choices, allowing visitors to indulge in the rich culinary heritage of Andalucia.

One of the highlights of the Feria de Abril is the stunning horse parades. Elegant riders, dressed in traditional attire, guide their beautifully adorned horses through the fairgrounds, showcasing the pride and elegance of Andalucian horsemanship. The horses are decorated with intricate braids, colorful ribbons, and adorned saddles, creating a mesmerizing sight for spectators. The riders, often in traditional Andalucian costumes, exude grace and poise as they navigate the fairgrounds, leaving onlookers in awe.

The Feria de Abril is a family-friendly event that offers entertainment for people of all ages. Children are treated to a variety of attractions and amusement rides, adding an extra layer of excitement to the fair. From thrilling Ferris wheels to exhilarating carousel rides, there are endless opportunities for laughter and fun. Traditional games and activities like ring-tossing, puppet shows, and face painting ensure that children have an unforgettable experience.

The festivities extend into the late hours of the night, as the atmosphere becomes even more lively and vibrant. The casetas continue to buzz with energy as live bands and DJs take to the stage, filling the air with infectious beats and melodies. The night becomes a whirlwind of dancing, laughter, and merriment, with people reveling in the joyous ambiance until the early hours of the morning.

Attending the Feria de Abril is not just an event; it is an immersive experience that allows visitors to fully immerse themselves in the rich cultural heritage of Andalucia. It is an opportunity to witness the genuine warmth and hospitality of the locals, as they open their casetas and hearts to welcome guests from near and far. Whether one is captivated by the mesmerizing flamenco performances, indulging in the delectable culinary offerings, or simply savoring the festive spirit that permeates every corner of the fairgrounds, the

Feria de Abril is an unforgettable celebration of Andalucia's traditions, spirit, and joie de vivre.

Semana Santa: Andalucia's Holy Week Celebrations

Semana Santa, or Holy Week, is a deeply significant event in Andalucia, both in terms of religious devotion and cultural heritage. This week-long celebration, leading up to Easter, immerses the cities of Andalucia, such as Seville, Granada, and Malaga, in a profound atmosphere of faith, beauty, and tradition. The streets come alive with elaborate processions, religious statues, and a palpable sense of devotion that captivates both locals and visitors alike.

The heart of Semana Santa lies in the processions, which are organized by religious brotherhoods known as "hermandades" or "cofradías." These brotherhoods have deep historical roots and play a central role in the festivities. Members of the brotherhoods, dressed in traditional robes, known as "nazarenos," embark on a solemn journey through the streets, carrying intricately crafted statues, or "pasos," depicting scenes from the Passion of Christ.

The processions are meticulously planned and executed, with each brotherhood following a precise schedule and route. The "pasos" are carried on enormous floats, often weighing several tons, and are borne on the shoulders of the dedicated members of the brotherhoods. These bearers, known as "costaleros," endure physical strain as they navigate through the city streets, guided by the rhythmic commands of their capataz, the leader of the group.

As the processions make their way through the labyrinthine streets, the atmosphere becomes electric with anticipation and reverence. Spectators line the streets, balconies, and windows, eager to catch a glimpse of the solemn pageantry. The processions move at a deliberate pace, accompanied by the haunting sounds of religious music played by brass bands. The rhythmic beats of drums, the mournful notes of trumpets, and the soul-stirring melodies of the orchestra create a poignant ambiance that resonates deep within the hearts of those present.

The streets themselves are transformed into a visual feast, adorned with vibrant floral displays and intricate decorations. Balconies are draped with richly colored fabrics, while the cobbled streets are carpeted with aromatic flowers, forming a fragrant path for the processions. The smell of incense permeates the air, adding an ethereal touch to the experience.

A unique aspect of Semana Santa is the tradition of the "saetas." These are passionate, improvised songs sung spontaneously from balconies or in the midst of the crowd, paying homage to the religious figures being carried in the processions. The saetas, with their flamenco-like melodies and heartfelt lyrics, express a deep connection to faith and serve as a form of spiritual communication between the people and the divine.

Each city in Andalucia has its own distinct Semana Santa traditions, with Seville being particularly renowned for its grand processions and breathtaking spectacle. In Seville, the streets are transformed into a theater of devotion, as thousands of people gather to witness the processions. The most iconic event of Seville's Semana Santa is the "Madrugá," the early hours of Good Friday, when some of the most solemn and awe-inspiring processions take place. Throughout the night, long lines of "nazarenos" and "pasos" wind their way through the narrow streets, creating an unforgettable visual spectacle.

Granada and Malaga also have their unique Semana Santa traditions. In Granada, the processions pass through the narrow and picturesque streets of the Albaicín neighborhood, creating a harmonious blend of religious fervor and historical charm. Malaga, with its coastal setting, offers a distinctive Semana Santa experience, where processions take place against the backdrop of the Mediterranean Sea, enhancing the dramatic effect.

Beyond the religious significance, Semana Santa is a time for families to come together and celebrate their shared heritage. It is a period when people reconnect with their traditions, participate in communal activities, and strengthen bonds with their community. Many families have been involved in the brotherhoods for generations, passing down the responsibility and honor of participating in the processions.

Semana Santa is a time of reflection, introspection, and spiritual renewal for the people of Andalucia. It serves as a reminder of the profound historical and cultural roots that have shaped the region. Through the processions, music, saetas, and decorations, the people of Andalucia express their faith, devotion, and respect for the traditions that have been passed down for centuries.

For visitors, Semana Santa offers a unique opportunity to witness and partake in this vibrant expression of faith and culture. It provides a window into the soul of Andalucia, allowing them to experience firsthand the devotion, beauty, and deep-rooted traditions that define the region. Semana Santa in Andalucia is a sensory and emotional journey that leaves a lasting impression on all who have the privilege of being a part of it.

The Cordoba Patio Festival: Floral Beauty and Tradition

The Cordoba Patio Festival, also known as Festival de los Patios, is a captivating event that captures the essence of Cordoba's vibrant culture and showcases the intrinsic beauty of its patios. This annual festival, held in May, offers visitors a remarkable opportunity to explore the hidden courtyards of Cordoba's historic homes, immersing themselves in a world of vibrant colors, aromatic scents, and traditional Andalucian decor.

As the festival unfolds, the normally private patios of Cordoba open their doors to the public, inviting visitors to embark on a journey of discovery. Stepping into these stunning spaces is like stepping into a different world, where nature and architecture blend harmoniously to create an enchanting ambiance. Each patio boasts a unique design, meticulously adorned with vibrant flowers, flourishing plants, and intricate details that reflect the rich cultural heritage of the region.

One of the most captivating aspects of the Cordoba Patio Festival is the exquisite decoration of the patios. Delicate hand-painted tiles, known as azulejos, embellish the walls, telling stories of the city's past. Ornate fountains, adorned with intricate mosaics, provide a soothing soundtrack of flowing water, adding to the tranquil atmosphere. Fragrant orange blossom trees, known as naranjos, fill the air with their sweet scent, creating a sensory experience that is both visually and aromatically captivating.

As you stroll through the narrow streets of Cordoba, you'll find yourself mesmerized by the hidden gems that await at every turn. The festival provides a rare glimpse into the private courtyards that have been lovingly maintained by generations of homeowners. It's a testament to the dedication and passion of the Cordobeses who work tirelessly to preserve this centuries-old tradition, ensuring that the beauty and cultural significance of the patios are celebrated and shared with the world.

In addition to the visual feast offered by the patios, the festival is a celebration of music, dance, and culinary delights. Live performances of traditional Andalucian music, including flamenco, fill the air with soul-stirring melodies and rhythms that evoke the spirit of the region. Professional dancers showcase their skill and passion, captivating audiences with their graceful movements and powerful expressions.

The Cordoba Patio Festival is also a gastronomic paradise, offering visitors the opportunity to savor local delicacies and traditional dishes. From savory tapas to mouthwatering desserts, the festival showcases the culinary delights of Andalucia. Indulge in regional specialties such as salmorejo, a creamy tomato soup garnished with ham and hard-boiled eggs, or try the refreshing local drink, rebujito, a mix of sherry wine and soda that perfectly complements the festive atmosphere.

Beyond the visual and gastronomic treats, the Cordoba Patio Festival is a celebration of community spirit and cultural heritage. The festival brings people together, fostering a sense of camaraderie and pride among the Cordobeses. It's a time when locals and visitors alike come together to appreciate the beauty that surrounds them and to honor the traditions that have shaped their city.

The festival serves as a reminder of the deep-rooted connection between nature, architecture, and community in Andalucia. The patios, with their flourishing flowers and intricate designs, symbolize the region's reverence for nature and its ability to enhance the built environment. They also embody the spirit of community, as homeowners generously open their doors to share their beloved patios with others, creating a sense of unity and belonging.

Attending the Cordoba Patio Festival is an unforgettable experience that offers a glimpse into the heart and soul of Andalucia. It's a celebration of beauty, creativity, and cultural heritage that will leave you with lasting memories. As you wander through the enchanting patios, surrounded by vibrant colors and the scent of blossoming flowers, you'll come to understand why this festival holds such a special place in the hearts of Cordobeses and visitors alike.

Wanderlust in Andalucia: Uncover Hidden Gems and Local Secrets

Off the Beaten Path: Andalucia's Hidden Villages

When it comes to exploring Andalucia, the well-known cities like Seville, Granada, and Cordoba often steal the spotlight. However, nestled within the region are countless hidden villages that hold their own charm and allure. These lesser-known gems provide an authentic experience and offer a glimpse into the heart and soul of Andalucian culture and traditions. In this chapter, we invite you to venture off the beaten path and discover the picturesque and enchanting villages that are waiting to be explored.

One such region that boasts a collection of captivating hidden villages is the Alpujarras. Tucked away in the southern slopes of the Sierra Nevada mountain range, the Alpujarras is known for its stunning natural landscapes and traditional white-washed villages. Take a leisurely stroll through Pampaneira, Bubion, and Capileira, where the narrow streets are lined with charming houses adorned with colorful flower pots. Immerse yourself in the laid-back atmosphere as you interact with friendly locals and savor the traditional Alpujarran cuisine, known for its hearty stews and locally sourced ingredients. The Alpujarras offers a serene escape from the bustling cities, allowing you to connect with nature and experience the genuine warmth of Andalucian hospitality.

As you journey further, you'll come across the hilltop towns of Grazalema and Zahara de la Sierra. These villages, perched high on cliffs, offer breathtaking panoramic views of the surrounding countryside. Grazalema, known for its traditional whitewashed houses and narrow streets, is nestled within a natural park and is a haven for nature lovers and hikers. Embark on a scenic hike through the Sierra de Grazalema Natural Park, home to diverse flora and fauna, including the rare Pinsapo fir trees. The village itself exudes tranquility, inviting you to unwind in its charming squares and savor the local delicacies in its quaint restaurants.

Zahara de la Sierra, another hidden treasure, sits atop a steep hill overlooking a beautiful turquoise reservoir. Its iconic castle ruins stand as a testament to its rich history and strategic importance. Explore the cobbled streets and discover the unique Moorish and medieval architecture that adorns the village. As you wander through its alleyways, you'll stumble upon hidden courtyards, vibrant flower displays, and traditional artisan shops. A visit to Zahara de la Sierra offers an opportunity to step back in time and soak in the ambiance of this enchanting village.

While the Alpujarras and Grazalema-Zahara de la Sierra region showcase the beauty of Andalucia's hidden villages, they are just a glimpse of what awaits. Throughout the region, you'll find countless other villages that each have their own distinctive character and allure. From the whitewashed town of Frigiliana with its labyrinthine streets adorned with colorful ceramics, to the medieval village of Arcos de la Frontera perched atop a rocky ridge, there are endless hidden treasures waiting to be discovered.

What makes these villages truly special is the opportunity to connect with the locals and immerse yourself in their way of life. Step into a local tavern and strike up a conversation with the friendly villagers. You'll find that they are eager to share stories of their village's history, traditions, and customs. Whether it's witnessing age-old artisanal crafts being practiced or partaking in a traditional festival, you'll gain insight into the authentic traditions that have shaped these communities for generations.

As you explore these hidden villages, take the time to appreciate the breathtaking landscapes that surround them. Andalucia's diverse geography offers a range of natural wonders, from rolling hills and fertile valleys to rugged mountains and pristine coastlines. Each village has its own unique setting, offering opportunities for outdoor adventures such as hiking, biking, or simply taking a leisurely stroll through nature. Capture the essence of Andalucia as you wander along ancient footpaths, breathe in the scent of wildflowers, and listen to the soothing sounds of nature.

The hidden villages of Andalucia also provide a glimpse into the region's rich history. From Roman and Moorish influences to medieval fortresses and Baroque churches, the architectural treasures found in these villages tell stories of centuries past. Explore the ancient ruins, visit historical sites, and marvel at the craftsmanship of the local artisans who have preserved their cultural heritage.

The hidden villages of Andalucia offer a captivating alternative to the well-trodden tourist path. By venturing beyond the popular cities and exploring these picturesque and lesser-known villages, you'll uncover the region's authentic charm, rich history, and breathtaking landscapes. From the white-washed villages of the Alpujarras to the hilltop towns of Grazalema and Zahara de la Sierra, each village holds its own allure and provides a unique experience. So, pack your bags, put on your walking shoes, and get ready to embark on a journey of discovery through Andalucia's hidden gems.

Insider Tips for Authentic Experiences

To truly experience Andalucia like a local, it's essential to go beyond the typical tourist attractions and delve into the heart of the region's vibrant culture. This chapter aims to provide insider tips and recommendations for authentic experiences that will allow you to immerse yourself in the true essence of Andalucia. By mingling with locals, participating in traditional festivals and events, and engaging in various activities, you'll gain a deeper understanding of the rich traditions, customs, and way of life in this captivating region.

One of the best ways to connect with locals and experience the authentic spirit of Andalucia is by visiting bustling markets. These vibrant hubs of activity are not only a treasure trove of fresh produce, local crafts, and unique products but also a meeting point for locals to socialize and connect. Explore markets like Mercado de Triana in Seville or Mercado de Atarazanas in Malaga, where you can wander through stalls, engage in friendly conversations with vendors, and sample regional delicacies. From savoring the intense flavors of local olives and cheeses to selecting the freshest fruits and vegetables, the markets offer an immersive and sensory experience that reflects the true essence of Andalucia.

Participating in traditional festivals and events is another fantastic way to embrace the vibrant culture of Andalucia. Throughout the year, the region comes alive with a myriad of festivities, each with its unique traditions and rituals. From the grand Semana Santa processions in Seville to the colorful Feria de Abril, where locals gather to dance Sevillanas and celebrate, these events offer a glimpse into the deep-rooted traditions that define Andalucian life. Attend the local Romerías (pilgrimages) that take place in various towns, where you can join the lively processions, witness traditional attire, and partake in festive music and dance. By immersing yourself in these celebrations, you'll gain a profound appreciation for the cultural heritage and passionate spirit of the Andalucian people.

For those seeking to explore the arts and immerse themselves in the soul-stirring rhythms of Andalucia, learning flamenco is an absolute must. This passionate and expressive dance form is deeply ingrained in the region's cultural fabric. Find a local dance studio or academy where you can take flamenco lessons and learn the intricate footwork, graceful hand movements, and emotional nuances of this captivating art form. Not only will you gain insight into the essence of Andalucia's music and dance, but you'll also experience the joy of expressing yourself through the power of flamenco.

Andalucia's culinary scene is renowned for its delectable tapas and flavorful dishes. To fully indulge in the local gastronomy, venture beyond tourist hotspots and seek out neighborhood taverns and bars where locals gather. These hidden culinary gems serve up traditional Andalucian tapas bursting with flavors. Sit at the bar, strike up a conversation with the bartender or fellow patrons, and savor an array of small plates, each showcasing the region's culinary heritage. From succulent jamón ibérico and fresh seafood to mouthwatering patatas bravas and gazpacho, every bite will transport you deeper into the culinary soul of Andalucia.

To delve even deeper into the culinary traditions, consider joining a local cooking class. These immersive experiences allow you to learn directly from passionate chefs who are eager to share their knowledge and techniques. Discover the secrets of creating the perfect paella or mastering the art of making traditional Andalucian gazpacho. Engage in hands-on preparation using locally sourced ingredients, and gain valuable insights into the history, flavors, and techniques that make Andalucian cuisine so exceptional. Not only will you expand your culinary skills, but you'll also forge connections with locals who are passionate about their gastronomic heritage.

In addition to these specific recommendations, it's important to embrace the spontaneity of your journey and be open to unexpected encounters and experiences. Strike up conversations with locals you meet along the way, whether it's a friendly shopkeeper, a fellow traveler, or a proud Andalucian. They can provide valuable insights, share hidden gems, and offer personal recommendations that are not found in guidebooks. The warmth and hospitality of the Andalucian people are contagious, and their stories and perspectives will enrich your travel experience.

Remember to venture off the beaten path and explore the lesser-known neighborhoods, villages, and countryside. Take leisurely walks through charming streets, get lost in the narrow alleys, and stumble upon hidden plazas where locals gather. By immersing yourself in the daily rhythm of life, you'll discover authentic moments and encounters that truly capture the essence of Andalucia.

Experiencing Andalucia like a local is about embracing the vibrant culture, traditions, and way of life that define this captivating region. By mingling with locals at bustling markets, participating in traditional festivals and events, learning flamenco, indulging in tapas at neighborhood taverns, joining cooking classes, and being open to unexpected encounters, you'll unlock a deeper understanding of Andalucia's soul. These insider tips and recommendations will enhance your journey, create lasting memories, and leave you with a profound appreciation for the rich heritage and warm hospitality of Andalucia.

Unique Souvenirs to Bring Home

When it comes to souvenirs, Andalucia embraces a rich cultural heritage that is beautifully reflected in its unique and distinctive handcrafted products. This chapter will take you on a journey through the treasure trove of Andalucian souvenirs, allowing you to explore the diverse range of items that capture the essence of the region.

One of the most renowned artisanal crafts in Andalucia is ceramics. The region boasts a long and storied tradition of pottery-making, with each city and village adding its own distinct style to the art form. From the vibrant blue and white patterns of traditional Sevillian ceramics to the intricate geometric designs of Granada's Fajalauza pottery, you'll discover a world of exquisite craftsmanship. Whether you choose a decorative plate, a hand-painted tile, or a beautifully glazed vase, these ceramics will bring a touch of Andalucian elegance to your home.

Textiles also play a significant role in Andalucian craftsmanship, showcasing the region's rich history of weaving and embroidery. In places like Ronda and Alpujarra, you'll find stunning handwoven rugs and blankets, skillfully crafted using traditional techniques. These textiles often feature vibrant colors and intricate patterns inspired by the natural surroundings and cultural heritage of the area. By selecting one of these textiles as a souvenir, you not only acquire a beautiful and functional item but also support local artisans and the preservation of age-old weaving traditions.

No exploration of Andalucian souvenirs would be complete without mentioning the region's liquid gold – olive oil. Andalucia is known for its exceptional olive oil production, with groves dotting the landscape as far as the eye can see. The local olives are carefully harvested and cold-pressed to produce high-quality extra virgin olive oil that is sought after around the world. Consider bringing home a bottle of this liquid gold, which not only adds incredible flavor to your dishes but also serves as a reminder of Andalucia's vast olive-growing heritage.

Flamenco, the soul-stirring dance and music form that originated in Andalucia, holds a special place in the hearts of locals. Embrace the spirit of flamenco by acquiring traditional flamenco accessories as souvenirs. From intricately designed castanets to handcrafted fans adorned with delicate lacework, these items capture the passion and elegance of this iconic art form. Whether you choose to display them as decorative pieces or try your hand at flamenco rhythms, these accessories will forever remind you of the fiery essence of Andalucia.

Beyond ceramics, textiles, olive oil, and flamenco accessories, Andalucia offers a myriad of other unique souvenirs. Delve into the world of leather goods, where you can find exquisite handbags, wallets, and belts crafted by skilled artisans in cities like Ubrique. The delicate art of filigree jewelry is another local specialty, with artisans meticulously shaping gold or silver wire into intricate designs inspired by nature and Andalucian motifs. And if you're a lover of traditional Spanish cuisine, consider bringing home some saffron, pimentón (smoked paprika), or Iberian ham, prized delicacies that reflect the region's gastronomic excellence.

When selecting souvenirs in Andalucia, it's not just about acquiring objects; it's about embracing the spirit and artistry of the region. Each handcrafted item tells a story and carries the heritage of the craftsmen who devoted their skills and passion to create it. By choosing these meaningful souvenirs, you become part of a centuries-old tradition and contribute to the preservation of Andalucia's cultural legacy.

As you wander through Andalucia's markets, craft shops, and artisanal boutiques, take the time to engage with the local artisans. They are often eager to share their knowledge, skills, and stories, providing a deeper appreciation for the artistry behind each piece. Learning about the craftsmanship and the cultural significance of these souvenirs enhances their value and creates a stronger connection between you and the region.

Andalucia's souvenirs offer a remarkable array of handcrafted products and traditional crafts that capture the essence of the region. From the exquisite ceramics and vibrant textiles to the locally produced olive oil and traditional flamenco accessories, each item tells a story and reflects the spirit and artistry of Andalucia. By selecting these unique souvenirs, you not only acquire beautiful mementos of your Andalucian adventure but also support local artisans and contribute to the preservation of Andalucia's cultural heritage. So, as you explore the markets and shops, allow yourself to be inspired and guided by the rich artistic tapestry of Andalucia, and bring home a piece of its captivating beauty.

Andalucia's Best-Kept Secrets: Unraveling Local Legends and Mysteries

Andalucia, with its rich history and diverse cultural heritage, is a land teeming with legends, folklore, and mysterious tales. These captivating stories have been passed down through generations, immersing the region in an aura of mystique and enchantment. In this chapter, we invite you to delve into the hidden stories and secrets that surround Andalucia, unlocking the intriguing mysteries that lie beneath its surface.

One of the most iconic landmarks in Andalucia is the Alhambra, a magnificent palace and fortress complex in Granada. Legends shroud the Alhambra, adding an air of intrigue to its already awe-inspiring beauty. As you explore its exquisite architecture and lush gardens, you'll encounter tales of love, betrayal, and secrets whispered within its walls. From the haunting legends of the ghostly princesses of the Alhambra to the hidden passages rumored to lead to hidden treasures, each story adds another layer of fascination to this UNESCO World Heritage site.

Venturing further into the rugged landscapes of the Sierra Nevada mountain range, another world awaits—a realm of mythical creatures and legendary tales. The Sierra Nevada is home to stories of the Moorish jinn, mischievous and shape-shifting spirits that are said to inhabit the mountains. These mystical beings, woven into the fabric of Andalucian folklore, add an element of magic and wonder to the natural beauty of the region. Exploring the Sierra Nevada's peaks, valleys, and pristine lakes, you may find yourself captivated by the lingering presence of these mythical creatures, hidden in the misty folds of the mountains.

Beyond the realm of legends, Andalucia holds ancient mysteries within its megalithic sites. These prehistoric structures, such as dolmens and menhirs, offer a glimpse into the distant past and raise intriguing questions about the lives and beliefs of the people who constructed them. As you venture into the countryside, you'll discover the enigmatic Dolmen de Menga in Antequera, an awe-inspiring megalithic monument that dates back over 5,000 years. Standing in its presence, you can't help but wonder about the rituals, ceremonies, and ancient practices that took place within its stone chambers.

Andalucian architecture itself is imbued with hidden symbolism and meaning, telling stories that transcend time. From the intricate carvings of the Alhambra to the grand cathedrals and mosques scattered throughout the region, every arch, column, and detail carries significance. Unraveling the symbolism in Andalucian architecture reveals a tapestry of cultural exchange, religious influences, and historical events. The interplay of Islamic, Christian, and Jewish architectural elements reflects the complex history of Andalucia, a land where different cultures once coexisted and left their indelible marks.

As you embark on a journey of discovery, you'll encounter these tales and secrets that have shaped Andalucia's history and culture. Local guides and storytellers will share the stories passed down through generations, allowing you to glimpse the region's hidden narratives. Whether it's sitting in a cozy tavern in the winding streets of Cordoba, where stories of lost love and heroism come alive, or joining a guided tour of the ancient ruins of Baelo Claudia, where Roman legends intertwine with the power struggles of empires, each step deepens your understanding of Andalucia's rich tapestry of stories.

Unveiling the legends and mysteries of Andalucia adds an extra layer of enchantment to your journey. It invites you to see the region through the eyes of those who came before, to imagine the lives they lived and the stories they shared. As you explore the landscapes, monuments, and hidden corners of Andalucia, let the stories guide you, infusing your experience with a sense of wonder and connection to the past. From the Alhambra to the Sierra Nevada, from megalithic sites to architectural wonders, Andalucia's hidden tales await, ready to captivate your imagination and leave an indelible mark on your journey.

By exploring the hidden villages, seeking authentic experiences, selecting unique souvenirs, and unraveling local legends and mysteries, you'll embark on a truly immersive and unforgettable journey through Andalucia. These chapters will guide you off the beaten path, allowing you to connect with the soul of the region and create cherished memories that will last a lifetime.

Conclusion

In conclusion, the Andalucia Travel Guide has been meticulously crafted to serve as your ultimate companion on a comprehensive and insightful journey through the captivating region of Andalucia, located in the southern part of Spain. Throughout the chapters of this guide, we have endeavored to unlock the essence of Andalucia by delving into its rich history, vibrant culture, architectural wonders, gastronomic delights, natural landscapes, and hidden gems.

By immersing yourself in the pages of this guide, you have embarked on a voyage of discovery, unearthing the layers of Andalucia's past and present. You have traversed the annals of time, tracing the footsteps of ancient civilizations that have left indelible marks on the region's heritage. From the remnants of Moorish influence to the echoes of Roman and Phoenician civilizations, you have witnessed the tapestry of history woven into the fabric of Andalucia.

Moreover, this guide has allowed you to unravel the vibrant tapestry of Andalucian culture. You have experienced the passion and intensity of flamenco, a soul-stirring dance form that serves as a window into the region's emotions and traditions. You have savored the exquisite flavors of Andalucia's gastronomy, indulging in the fusion of Moorish, Mediterranean, and Spanish influences that create a tantalizing culinary experience. From sipping a glass of sherry in Jerez to savoring traditional tapas in Granada, you have embraced the flavors that make Andalucia a true gastronomic paradise.

Andalucia's architectural wonders have also revealed themselves through the pages of this guide. You have marveled at the intricate details of the Alhambra in Granada, a breathtaking testament to Islamic architecture. You have wandered through the winding streets of Cordoba's historic center, where the Great Mosque stands as a symbol of religious and architectural harmony. From the Royal Alcazar in Seville to the awe-inspiring Puente Nuevo in Ronda, you have witnessed the grandeur and beauty of Andalucia's architectural gems.

In addition to its cultural and historical treasures, Andalucia boasts an abundance of natural landscapes that beckon the adventurous traveler. From the snow-capped peaks of the Sierra Nevada to the sun-kissed beaches of the Costa del Sol, you have discovered the diverse and awe-inspiring natural wonders that Andalucia has to offer. By exploring its national parks, hiking trails, and coastal havens, you have immersed yourself in the untamed beauty of Andalucia's outdoors, creating memories that will last a lifetime.

By delving into the chapters of this guide, you have not only gained a deeper understanding of Andalucia's soul but also acquired valuable information to plan an unforgettable trip. From practical tips for navigating transportation systems to recommendations for accommodations and itineraries, this guide has equipped you with the necessary tools to make the most of your time in Andalucia. Whether you seek a cultural immersion, an epicurean adventure, or a rendezvous with nature, the Andalucia Travel Guide has provided the insights and guidance to shape your travel experience into a truly remarkable one.

As you bid farewell to the pages of this guide, we encourage you to go forth and explore Andalucia with an open heart and an adventurous spirit. Immerse yourself in the warmth of its people, soak in the vibrant atmosphere of its festivals, and let the timeless beauty of the region captivate your senses. Andalucia awaits, ready to unveil its treasures and create memories that will forever be etched in your heart. Safe travels, and may your journey through Andalucia be nothing short of extraordinary.

Appendix: Useful Resources and Further Reading:

As you continue your exploration of Andalucia, there are various resources available to enhance your travel experience and provide you with valuable information and assistance. Here are some recommendations:

Official Tourism Websites:

Visiting the official websites of Andalucia's tourism boards is a great starting point for gathering the latest updates, maps, itineraries, and travel recommendations. These websites often provide comprehensive information about the region's attractions, accommodations, transportation options, and upcoming events. They are valuable resources for planning your itinerary and ensuring you have access to accurate and up-to-date information throughout your journey.

Online Forums and Communities:

Engaging with fellow travelers and locals on online forums and communities adds a dynamic and interactive dimension to your Andalucian adventure. Platforms such as TripAdvisor, Lonely Planet's Thorn Tree Forum, and Reddit's r/Andalucia are excellent places to seek advice, share experiences, and discover insider tips. You can ask specific questions, read others' travel stories, and find recommendations for accommodations, restaurants, attractions, and off-the-beaten-path destinations. These communities are often filled with passionate individuals who are eager to help and share their firsthand knowledge of Andalucia.

Mobile Apps:

In the digital age, travel apps have become indispensable tools for travelers. When exploring Andalucia, make use of popular travel apps such as Google Maps, TripAdvisor, and Airbnb. Google Maps is excellent for navigating the region, finding directions, and locating attractions and services. TripAdvisor provides user reviews and ratings for accommodations, restaurants, and activities, helping you make informed decisions. Airbnb offers a range of unique accommodations, allowing you to experience the local culture and hospitality. These mobile apps offer convenience, real-time information, and recommendations on-the-go, enhancing your travel experience in Andalucia.

Language Resources:

To enhance your interactions and experiences in Andalucia, consider learning some basic Spanish phrases. While English is spoken in many tourist areas, having a basic grasp of the local language can go a long way in connecting with the locals, understanding the culture, and navigating daily situations. Language learning platforms such as Duolingo, Babbel, and Rosetta Stone offer user-friendly courses that can help you learn Spanish at your own pace. Even a few key phrases and expressions can greatly enrich your travel experience, as locals often appreciate the effort and it can lead to memorable encounters and deeper cultural immersion.